SCHOOL WAS OUR LIFE

COUNTERPOINTS: MUSIC AND EDUCATION

Estelle R. Jorgensen, *Editor*

SCHOOL WAS OUR LIFE

OUR LIFE

Remembering Progressive Education

Jane Roland Martin

Foreword by Estelle R. Jorgensen

Indiana University Press

This book is a publication of

Indiana University Press
Office of Scholarly Publishing
Herman B Wells Library 350
1320 East 10th Street
Bloomington, Indiana 47405 USA

iupress.indiana.edu

The paper used in this publication meets the minimum requirements of
the American National Standard for Information Sciences—Permanence
of Paper for Printed Library Materials, ANSI Z39.48-1992.

Manufactured in the United States of America

Cataloging information is available from the Library of Congress.

ISBN 978-0-253-03301-7 (cloth)
ISBN 978-0-253-03302-4 (paperback)
ISBN 978-0-253-03303-1 (ebook)

1 2 3 4 5   23 22 21 20 19 18

In Memory
  Elisabeth Antoinette Irwin (1880–1942)
  "Mother of our youth"

Contents

Contents

Foreword

Estelle R. Jorgensen

JANE ROLAND MARTIN's *School Was Our Life: Remembering Progressive Education* opens a different perspective on music education for readers of the *Counterpoints: Music and Education* series. Teachers, students, and parents will be familiar with her situated picture of musical and artistic education as a part of public school education. Much music education writing focuses on aspects of music teaching, learning, instruction, curriculum, and administration that too often are considered independently of other subjects and exist on the margins of general education and schooling. Martin adds an important dimension to the literature on music and the arts in education by viewing them contextually rather than apart from the rest of general education. She writes with a broad perspective on culture and schools. Her memories and those of her classmates are clearly musical and poetic yet her present focus is on schooling and its connectedness to the rest of life. The arts emerge throughout her narrative in conjunction with other subjects, sometimes incidentally and other times focally. Sometimes, they assist in learning and retaining other subject matter and other times they are interesting and meaningful for their own sake.

Progressive educational and artistic ideas are enjoying something of a renaissance in our time along with a renewed interest in the writings of John Dewey. Martin pictures progressive education for us as she reflects on her experience and that of her fellow classmates at Little Red, an independent school in New York City. Here we see the school through the eyes of these students as they recall their school experiences and reflect on what this education means to them toward the end of their lives. True, memory can play tricks on one and the passage of time can romanticize what really occurred. Still, this school powerfully impacted the lives of its students. There are high points of shared experience in the confluence of detailed memories and stories of their schooling and its integration with the rest of life. What is remembered after the passage of decades into old age represents "the remainder" after unimportant details have been forgotten. Martin's account reveals the humanity of teachers and students in the school. It illustrates ways in which John Dewey's hopes for an education that integrates school and life, the arts and other curricular subjects, the subject matter and the students, and notions of freedom and social control could be realized.[1] At a time when public school teachers in American public schools too often find themselves beleaguered, it is inspiring to read Martin's narrative of hopeful and humane schooling, in which students feel cherished, teachers love their subjects and their students, and the school is led by an enlightened principal.

Not surprisingly, Martin and her classmates feel fortunate to have received a rich education in things that mattered to them for the rest of their lives. Theirs was an emotionally, physically, and intellectually engaging education. The stickiness of the songs and poems that they learned by heart is extraordinary when one considers that more than seven decades have passed since they attended this school. Educators, and especially teachers of the arts, will want to understand what sort of education would prompt a life-long result. I visited with Martin during the time that she was completing this book. A grand piano sits in her living room with musical scores on it. The song book that music teacher Mrs. Landeck compiled for her students is still treasured by Martin's former classmate Henry, and I count it a privilege to peruse his beautifully preserved copy. Thinking of a musical education that lasts makes me wish that every young person could remember the songs taught in elementary school with such relish and for so long. This is education that has clearly mattered to its participants in fundamental ways for a lifetime. Martin's book prompts educators in all subjects to reflect on how our present work can have this powerful impact and how it might be undertaken in ways that seep deeply into the souls of all of its participants.

It is revealing to come unexpectedly upon the early work of Beatrice Landeck Marks (1904–1978) before she became a noted music educator and compiler and editor of American folk songs for school use. Decades before Zoltán Kodály popularized the use of folk songs in music for the young,[2] Landeck had made folksongs (including those from people of

Native American, Mexican, and African heritage) a staple of her song curriculum. According to her daughter Olga Landeck Rothschild, "It was at Spring Hill [Connecticut] under the influence of Mabel Spinney that Beatrice became interested in folk music." Later, "She and Elisabeth Irwin traveled extensively in summers across the United States, collecting folk material and music."[3] Despite her pioneering music educational and ethnomusicological work, her contributions to music and progressive education have been largely overlooked in music educational scholarship of the period. Although she is mentioned in Sondra Wieland Howe's *Women Music Educators in the United States: A History* as a lead editor of a widely used basal series for school use in grades 1–8 entitled, *Making Music Your Own*, published by Silver Burdett, her work deserves greater attention.[4] Her publications include folk song compilations and books such as *"Git On Board": Collection of Folk Songs Arranged for Mixed Chorus, Songs My True Love Sings, Songs to Grow On: A Collection of American Folk Songs for Children, Children and Music: An Informal Guide for Parents and Teachers, More Songs to Grow On: A New Collection of Folk Songs for Children, Echoes of Africa in Folk Songs of the Americas,* and *Learn to Read: Read to Learn: Poetry and Prose from Afro-rooted Sources*; coedited books in the *Music for Living* series with James Mursell, Gladys Tipton, Harriet Nordholm, Roy Freeburg, and Jack Watson, including *I Like the City* and *Music Around the World*; a coauthored book with Elizabeth Crook, *Wake Up and Sing! Songs from America's Grass Roots*; several journal articles in the *Music Educators Journal*; and a chapter on music in Agnes De Lima's *The Little Red School House*.[5] Her music educational ideas were already taking shape in the songs she taught to her students at Little Red. As a progressive music teacher, her belief in the importance of finding songs that are like molasses and stick with people and her attention to repertoire and artistic performance as crucial elements of the musical education are already clear in her early public school music teaching.

Quite apart from what may be learned in this book about the intersection of school and life and the remembering of a past educational moment, educational researchers can benefit from reflecting on Martin's cross-disciplinary methodological approach to this study. Qualitative research relies on a researcher's intuitive grasp of a situation, in this case, that of a participant in the events described. It necessitates making meaning of the data in thoughtful and imaginative ways and writing a descriptive and evocative account that brings the subject matter alive for readers. Philosophy looms large over the investigation. As Martin invites us to imagine with her this remembrance of her life at school and school as life, we grasp the possibilities of going beyond telling a story, important as that may be, to exemplifying an educational practice that is humane, inclusive, holistic, experiential, life changing, and inspirational.

Notes

1. See John Dewey, Art and Experience, *Democracy and Education: An Introduction to the Philosophy of Education* ([1916]; repr., New York: Free Press, 1944); his *Art as Experience* ([1934]; repr., New York: G. P. Putnam's Sons, 1979); and his *Experience and Education* ([1938]; repr., New York: Collier Books, 1963).

2. See Zoltán Kodály, *The Selected Writings of Zoltán Kodály*, edited by Ferenc Bónis, translated by Lili Halápy and Fred Macnicol. London: Boosey and Hawkes, 1974.

3. Olga Landeck Rothschild, email communication to the author, April 21, 2017.

4. Sondra Wieland Howe, *Women Music Educators in the United States: A History* (Lanham, MD: Scarecrow Press, 2013). Also, see her "A Historical View of Women in Music Education Careers," *Philosophy of Music Education Review* 17, No. 2 (Fall 2009): 162–183.

5. See Beatrice Landeck, comp. and ed.,*"Git On Board": Collection of Folk Songs Arranged for Mixed Chorus* (New York: Edward B. Marks Music Corp, 1944); comp., *Songs My True Love Sings* (New York: Edward B. Marks Music Corp., 1946); *Songs to Grow On: A Collection of American Folk Songs for Children* (New York: E. B. Marks Music Corp., c1950); *Children and Music: An Informal Guide for Parents and Teachers* (New York: Sloane, 1952); *More Songs to Grow On: A New Collection of Folk Songs for Children* (New York: E. B. Marks Music Corp., 1954); *Echoes of Africa in Folk Songs of the Americas,* (New York: D. McKay, c1961), and *Learn to Read: Read to Learn: Poetry and Prose from Afro-rooted Sources* (New York: McKay, 1975); her coedited books including, James L. Mursell, Gladys Tipton, Beatrice Landeck, Harriet Nordholm, Roy E. Freeburg and Jack M. Watson, eds., *I Like the City*, Music for Living (Morristown, NJ: Silver Burdett, 1956), and James L. Mursell, Gladys Tipton, Harriet Nordholm, Roy E. Freeburg, Beatrice Landeck, and Jack M. Watson, eds., *Music Around the World*, Music for Living (Morristown, NJ: Silver Burdett, 1956) a coauthored book with Elizabeth Crook, *Wake Up and Sing! Songs from America's Grass Roots* (New York: E. B. Marks Music Corp., c1969); her articles including, "Standards of Literature and Performance in the Primary Level," *Music Educators Journal* 43, No. 2 (1956): 54–56, "Basic Ideas in Elementary Music," *Music Educators Journal* 50, No. 4 (1964): 67–68+70, and "A Happy Alternative to Embracing Rock," *Music Educators Journal* 55, No. 4 (1968): 35–36; and her chapter on music in Agnes De Lima's *The Little Red School House* (New York: Macmillan, 1942) available at https://archive.org/stream/littleredschoolho09715mbp/littleredschoolho09715mbp_djvu.txt.

Acknowledgments

MY THANKS GO first and foremost to my classmates for giving the interviews that ground this book. Next in line are Helena Ragoné and the late Mary Woods for conducting the interviews, and the Spencer Foundation for supporting the first round of interviews under its Small Grants Program. I am also grateful beyond words to Florence Freed, Janet Giele, Jane Williams, and Maurice Stein for reading and commenting on the first draft of this book; Beebe Nelson and Duncan Nelson for going over that manuscript with a fine-tooth comb; Daniel Mulcahy and Tim Reagan for asking me to present my work at the 2012 meeting of the New England Philosophy of Education Society; the AHA committee at Brookhaven in Lexington for inviting me to speak in 2014 about us lucky ones; Leonard Waks for allowing me to present chapter 3 at the John Dewey Society's 2016 Centennial Conference on Democracy and Education in Washington, DC; and The MacDowell Colony for the priceless gift in the summer of 2016 of a studio in the woods and a magically congenial environment in which to finish this volume. Michael Martin died before my work was done, but he accompanied me to our very first class reunion, attended several succeeding ones, and saw for himself that we were indeed the lucky ones. I dedicate this book to Elisabeth Irwin, in memory. As the song we sang at her memorial said and as the interviews testify, she truly was the mother of our youth.

SCHOOL WAS OUR LIFE

Introduction

THE STORY I tell here took place long ago. I enter the scene the September day I ride the subway down to the Little Red School House in New York City's Greenwich Village for the first time. It is two months after my tenth birthday and a week or two after the start of World War II. My tale begins earlier, however. An obvious starting point is 1934, the year my Little Red School House class—the "we" of this volume—came into existence. Yet back into history one can go.

The school opened in 1932 when the New York City Board of Education discontinued its funding of Elisabeth Irwin's experimental classes at P.S. 41. It was the height of the Great Depression, and according to one observer, "the world needed bread, not experiments in progressive education" (De Lima 1942, 210). And so, the P.S. 41 parents met in an ice cream parlor on Sixth Avenue "to mourn, perhaps or possibly, at the most, to appeal or to protest" (De Lima 1942, 211). There a butcher rose to his feet to say that he would contribute $5.00 a week to keep his children in Miss Irwin's classes. Other parents offered $2.00 or bread for lunches or their help as aides and voilà, the "Little Red" I knew was born. Elisabeth Irwin had launched the public school experiment that ultimately became Little Red in 1921,[1] however, and John Dewey—the man whose philosophy of education greatly influenced her—published some of his most important ideas at the turn of the twentieth century. Besides, had Dewey not read Jean-Jacques Rousseau's great educational treatise *Emile*—first published in 1762—who knows what *his* thinking would have been like?

By happy coincidence I write exactly one hundred years after the publication of Dewey's magnum opus *Democracy and Education*. Like Dewey, I do so in the belief that America's schools have lost their way, but his solution is not mine. Dewey hoped his idea of school would be put into practice by the entire nation. I doubt that any single model of school can fit all children. Besides, the world has changed drastically since our schooldays.

In 2012, a prominent supporter of charter schools said, "Any sane person would ask 'What can we learn from the success of the best charter schools?' rather than attack them all." To this, a charter school critic replied, "Why can't we learn from the regular schools that work?" (Denby 2012, 73). I write in the belief that we can learn from the best charter schools and the best "regular" schools, the best public and the best private schools, the best parochial and the best independent schools—*and also from the best progressive schools of this nation's past.*

I have just been reading *The Magic Mountain.* In the foreword, Thomas Mann stresses the need when telling the story of his hero Hans Castorp to use verbs "whose tense is of the deepest past" (1996, xi). In this story, I find it necessary to mix up my verbs. Its protagonists—that is to say, my classmates and I—recall the distant past as if it were present. The spin-doctors who want you to believe that the United States has been there and done progressive education and it was a disaster seek to erase from memory the fatal flaws in the traditional school practices they cherish. And I, a philosopher of education and eternal optimist, write in the hope that the children of today and tomorrow will be as lucky in their schooling as I was in mine.

The back cover of my copy of *The Magic Mountain* says that Mann uses a sanatorium in the Swiss Alps devoted exclusively to sickness as a microcosm for prewar 1914 Europe. I use the Little Red of my childhood as a microcosm of one of the many experiments in education the United States undertook in the years between the two world wars. When I described *School Was Our Life* to a Japanese scholar whose field of expertise is American education, he could barely contain his excitement. "This will be an important document," he said. "You know, don't you, that you were at the Little Red School House when progressive education was at its height?" I knew that I entered Little Red in September 1939 and I knew that historian Lawrence Cremin, whose *The Transformation of the School* is the classic work on the subject, wrote that the progressive education movement in the United States reached "its high-water mark" just before World War II (1961, 324). But I had not put two and two together.

Mann's microcosm and mine are in a very real sense polar opposites. Not only is his fictional and mine actual, but the residents of his sanatorium spend a good deal of their time learning to die, whereas we children were being taught how to live. For many years, I have considered the day I took the Eighth Avenue train to Fourth Street for the first time as the moment my life began. At ten years old, I knew how to read and write and add two plus two. I did not, however, know about the Tigris and the

Euphrates, the Norman Conquest, the Magna Carta, the Gutenberg Bible, or the Triangular Trade. These I learned about at Little Red and that is the least of it. A woman in her late seventies recently told me that she had gone to Shady Hill, a progressive school in Cambridge, Massachusetts. Lowering her voice she then said, "And that is who I am." "I know what you mean," was my reply. "I went to The Little Red School House."

In Mann's book, time is a central presence. Memory is the intangible element in my story. These pages are about school's past, present, and future: who remembers and who does not, what is remembered and what is not, and whether the remembering matters. Like many stories, this one has a subplot. The fact is that instead of treating progressive education as a living legacy, mainstream America now regards it as a dead relic best forgotten. My subplot tells how this puzzling fall from grace could possibly have happened. These pages record what we subjects of Miss Irwin's experiment recollect and what histories of American education have forgotten to say about the kind of education Dewey, Francis W. Parker, Elisabeth Irwin, and many other school reformers envisioned, and they remind us of the misinformation that now distorts our nation's remembrance of education past.

Why do I consider my classmates and me, our schoolmates, and those kindred spirits who went to schools like Little Red "The Lucky Ones"? Over lunch the other day, a man who was at the Francis W. Parker School—a progressive school in Chicago—when I was at Little Red said to me, "One thing I think you should know is that school was my whole life." It was mine, too, and what a good life it was!

Peterborough, New Hampshire
September 2016

Note

1. The Little Red School House is still alive and well in Greenwich Village. This story is, however, about the school my classmates and I long ago knew firsthand. For a detailed account of the school's origins see Ohan (2009).

1   Remembering Little Red

Together Again

It is August 1989 and ten of us plus spouses are at Henry's house in Worcester, Massachusetts. This is the first time we have been together since May 27, 1943, the day we graduated from the eighth grade, and it is as if we have never been apart. In her memoir *Lost in Translation*, Eva Hoffman describes what it is like to meet her childhood friend from Poland after a seventeen-year interruption: "We look at each other with some disbelief. This vigorous, handsome man is somebody I don't know at all, but he carries within himself a person I once knew completely" (1989, 224). Her friend says, "Who are you? Sometimes you seem a woman, sometimes a little girl" (228). This is the way it is for us after a forty-six-year interruption.

We remember everything about Little Red: our teachers; Miss Irwin, our principal; June Camp. "Do you know about June Camp?" one of my classmates asks when she is interviewed three years later. "I *adored* it." "I think everybody, practically everybody, loved June Camp," comments another. "We were gone for the month, and we did have some instruction, you know, lessons and stuff, but we also had a lot of outdoor play. And when we first went it was too cold to swim but as it got warmer and warmer we had swimming and things," says a third.

At Henry's we sing "Casey Jones," "A Mighty Ship Was the Gundremar," and "Stenka Razin." "Stinking Raisin" is what we used to call the protagonist of the Russian folk song, and we laugh at how embarrassed we once were by the lyric "Proudly sailed the arrow BREASTED, Ships of Cossack yeomanry." "I remember the music as being special," one classmate tells her interviewer. "My memory is that we had it every day, that we learned a new song either every day or every week 'til we had this vast knowledge." Another says, "To know that many songs. I mean, I know people, today they said, 'How come you know all these songs?' and I said, 'We sang them in school.' So yea, that was a brilliant thing."

Mrs. Landeck was our music teacher, and Emily writes me a letter in which she says: "What a marvelous woman. I remember the lessons in conducting. I remember the grace with which she did everything." According to the liner notes for a CD of the songs we sang at Little Red, "For 75 years music has been the part of Little Red and Elisabeth Irwin's curriculum that bound everything together."

Sitting in a circle on Henry's lawn, we recite the opening lines of Alfred Noyes's "The Highwayman," William Blake's "Tiger, Tiger," Vachel Lindsay's "The Congo," and Edna St. Vincent Millay's "The Ballad of the Harp-Weaver." "I can still see us sitting around in a circle," one classmate informs her interviewer, "and Marvin asking 'Now, who likes poetry?' Nobody raised their hand: Who likes poetry. That's silly. Okay. So he said, 'Okay, I am going to read you some poetry,' and he read it, and it was just like opening a door. It was so beautiful." "Very early on in the year," says another classmate, "he [Mr. Marvin] announced that by the end of the year everyone in the class would have written at least one poem and there was a snort ... And he didn't react to that. But then he started reading poetry, and he read poetry and he read poetry, and people kept gathering around him. We didn't have to."

Over our potluck lunch, Sue tells us how much she still regrets missing the trip to the sugar refinery when we were eight years old, and I silently bemoan not yet being at Little Red when our class built the pueblo:

> We built a two-story pueblo in the classroom out of beams and card-board and so on, but you could actually climb up the ladder to the second floor. That was a lot of fun.

> We learned more about Indians by building those pueblos and teepees and learning some of the songs and the dances than if we just sat down and studied where the Iroquois were and where the Chippewas were.

> The pueblo that we built in the third grade, my god I'll never forget that. Memorable, absolutely wonderful. Pretending I was a Pueblo Indian and climbing up and down those ladders, my lord, it was wonderful.

The year after that first reunion, we convene at the school. Some more classmates are there, but for me the highlight is our walk through the 196 Bleecker Street building. When my father died, I found the February 1940 issue of the mimeographed Little Red *Bulletin* in his top dresser drawer.

In it was an article by him in which he wrote: "Physically the school is big, and inside it rambles. The Bleecker Street front is soft gray with bright tan at the base; the doors concede to redness. The total effect is warm and mellow, and inviting. Inside the place is livable and lived in. A homey charm pervades, and you feel you've been there before. The proportions are right; they neither dwarf nor constrict. I get this feeling about the doors: They do not so much shut off as connect."

My friends and I tour the building and in the room where we had Rhythms—a class I always dreaded—Clarence skips across the floor as to the manner born. I have always thought that everyone hated Rhythms and I am wrong. One man in my class tells his interviewer: "As an eleven I hated a class called Rhythms. It was a mixture of dancing and calisthenics, and I think I was one of the leaders of a revolt against that class. A bunch of us would not follow the teacher's instructions very well" and two are of the opinion that all the boys hated Rhythms. But a third says, "Of course the boys didn't want to do it, but she [the teacher] said, you know, run across, pretend you're shot. Oh, we loved that. So that big, physical stuff was good."

On our tour I spy the closet where Kathy and I used to hide during art periods and the office where Miss Irwin listened patiently to complaints. A classmate recounts one such incident:

> In the bathroom there was a big hole in the floor where a pipe had been once and as you walked down the stairs the paint was peeling and falling down and a couple of chunks once fell on our head. Two other students and I complained about it to Miss Beeman and she said "Why don't you go and speak to the principal?" ... So we said Okay, and we made an appointment and she [Miss Irwin] listened to us. We told her all our different things, and she thanked us very much. And the next day there was a repairman scraping, painting the ceiling and fixing the hole in the pipe ... It meant to me that I was somebody that could affect my life, could affect the surrounding in which I had to live. That there were adults in the world, and I had never experienced this, neither in any of my schooling nor at home, unfortunately, from adults in my life at home, where a child's word was important and would get results.

The third time around I decide to skip the reunion. As Mr. Marvin who came from Duluth, Minnesota, and was our teacher in what most schools call fifth grade but Little Red, grouping us according to age, called the 10s used to say: "Enough is too much." Then I learn that our classmate Natalie has died and I know I must go to New York. I am, by trade, a philosophy professor and education is my specialty. I have published several books on the subject and have just begun work on what will eventually become *Cultural Miseducation*. My new research has made me see that my schoolmates and I—or, rather, our memories—are a rich cultural resource.

For reasons that I have only come to understand in the course of writing this book, Little Red is scarcely mentioned in the standard histories of American education. The oversight is surprising, to say the least, for when I was there it was one of the best-known progressive schools in the country. In the years before World War I people trooped to Rome to see Maria Montessori's schools in action. During my childhood, they flocked to Greenwich Village to observe and study Miss Irwin's.[1] According to one of my classmates, "I remember then all these people who used to come and sit when we were in elementary school and sort of sit around the edge and take notes and stuff." In my memory, large groups of grownups filed into our classrooms and stood shoulder to shoulder along three of the four walls. Why are they watching us, I would wonder. What do they find so interesting?

What with the history books ignoring the experiment in education that Little Red conducted in Greenwich Village and few if any studies of progressive education examining their subject from the point of view of the people most affected—the children—our combined memories constitute an important portion of this nation's educational wisdom.[2] Natalie's death is much more than a stark reminder that my classmates and I will not live forever. It sounds the alarm that unless something is done soon to preserve our remembrance of our schooldays past, a significant quantity of our culture's wealth will disappear.

At this third reunion, twelve of us spend a glorious June afternoon at Café Vivaldi, a dimly lit Greenwich Village coffee house, our present lives, families, and careers all but forgotten as we recite poems, sing our songs, reminisce about trips by subway to the Egyptian wing of the Metropolitan Museum of Art, and share stories about learning to read. Henry's is the most dramatic.

He tells us that every year his anxious mother would say to Miss Irwin, "Henry still can't read" and Miss Irwin would reply, "Don't worry, Dorothy. Henry will read when he's ready." Every Christmas time Henry would visit his uncle in Boston. His uncle would ask, "Henry, can you read yet?" and Henry would sheepishly say "No." Then we are in the 9s—fourth grade. Christmas comes and Henry's uncle again puts the question. This time Henry says, "Yes." "Well," gasps the astonished uncle, "Can you read this?" Henry picks up the newspaper his uncle hands him and starts to read.

When it is time for us to leave Café Vivaldi and walk over to the school for the reunion dinner, Sue balks. "Allan will be there and he always used to tell me that my nose was running," she says. "It probably was, but I can't face that again." "Don't be silly," we reply. "That was fifty years ago." "Allan won't remember," I chime in. "Anyway, he's a doctor, so even if he does, he won't bring it up." Sue reluctantly joins our march down Bleecker Street, across 6th Avenue, and through those reddish doors into the school. There in the hallway where Miss Kearney—she of the gleaming blue-white hair—used to sit and greet us each morning is Allan. I have trouble reconciling this rather portly gentleman in an expensive blue suede jacket with the skinny boy I used to know. He has no difficulty remembering Sue. "Does your nose still run?" he asks.

One month later, I phone historian Patricia Graham for a second opinion. I need assurance that my classmates' memories of Little Red ought to be preserved. I tell her what a heady experience our reunions have been and wonder aloud if some sort of oral history should be done before we all die off. Graham, then president of the Spencer Foundation, encourages me to enlist the help of an experienced interviewer and apply to her foundation for one of their grants. I do so, and anthropologist Helena Ragoné and I receive a Spencer Foundation award that enables us to conduct and transcribe fifteen interviews with members of the Little Red School House class of '43. When the grant ends, my high school classmate Mary Woods—a social worker and the author of a widely used textbook on casework—offers to continue the interviewing where Ragoné left off. As a result, I have at my disposal the recorded school memories of thirty of us.

Memory, Oh Memory

The first time I read the transcripts of the interviews Ragoné conducted, I was transported back to Dinty Moore land. After college, I worked in the market research department of a New York City advertising agency where I had the dubious privilege of typing up reports of customer opinions of Electrolux vacuum cleaners, Johnny Mops, and Dinty Moore beef stew. The Dinty Moore questionnaire results are the ones I remember best: roughly one-half of the respondents to our questionnaire thought the canned beef stew had too many carrots and not enough beef and the other half thought it had enough beef and too few carrots.

Representing the affirmative in the Little Red School House class of '43's Grammar Controversy, one of my classmates recalls: "We had Miss Kneeland who taught us grammar and I really learned grammar so that when I went to high school and they were teaching grammar I knew it. And when I went to college in Freshman English and they were teaching grammar I knew it." Another tells Ragoné: "I remember studying grammar and I have contemporary friends now who went to public school who have no memory of learning any grammar and I loved that and it was very helpful later on when I studied languages in high school." The three of us representing the negative—I am one of them—simply say: "I never was taught grammar," "We had never studied grammar and punctuation," and "I mean grammar, forget it. Forget it."

According to the old nursery rhyme: "Some like it hot, some like it cold, Some like it in the pot nine days old." Well, some liked the Dinty Moore carrots and some liked the beef, and that was that. When, however, three of us remember that Little Red taught our class grammar and three remember that it did not teach our class grammar, our preferences are not the issue. At issue is what actually happened.[3] Now that I recall a hugely embarrassing event, I know which of us have truth on their side. It took place in the 13s—eighth grade—and everyone but me thought it extremely funny.

It is not my habit to seek help, but when Miss Kneeland asks every kid in the class to write a sentence with a preposition in it and I sit there for what seems an eternity and come up with nothing, I take the plunge. I go up to her and in all innocence say, "Miss Kneeland, I can't think of any sentence that has a preposition in it." This is not an easy thing to do, for Miss Kneeland is the one teacher in our school with a reputation as a disciplinarian. True, a man who entered our class in the 13s says, "I loved our eighth-grade teacher ... She was an extraordinary woman, very loving, very involved, she worked with you as an individual ... I found her warm. I found her stimulating." But someone else reports being "a little bit scared of her" and a third comments, "Unlike many progressive school teachers she was no nonsense. She wasn't there to win popularity contests, but she was very dignified and she expected a great deal of us."

First Miss Kneeland doubles over with laughter, next she puts her arm around me, and then she turns to the class and says, "Children, would you believe it! Jane just said to me, 'Miss Kneeland, I can't think of any sentence that has a preposition in it.' Who can tell me how many prepositions are in what she just said?" Hands shoot up.

Is this a false memory? A few years ago, I regaled a man who was two years behind me with my sad tale and he roared: "Miss Kneeland told us that story. Do you mean to say that *you* were that girl?" With his aid and the help of an essay by Bob Lilien who was three years ahead of us, my belated recollection sets the grammar record straight.

The Little Red School House—written by Agnes De Lima in collaboration with Miss Irwin, the staff, and a school parent and published by MacMillan in 1942—gives a detailed account of the school's philosophy and practices. John Dewey, generally agreed to be one of the most important philosophers of education in the history of the Western world, says in his introduction: "When one contrasts what is actually done in a school of the kind here reported upon with the criticisms passed upon progressive schools by those who urge return to ancient and outworn patterns, one can only feel that the former is the one which has its feet on the ground, which is realistic, while the latter is the one which is theoretical in the bad sense of the word, since it is far away from the earth on which we now live" (De Lima 1942, ix).

My yellow-paged copy of the De Lima book bears an inscription to my father "for appreciation of his loyal friendship to the school" signed by Elisabeth Irwin on January 26, 1942. The chapter entitled "Our Graduates" contains an essay that Bob Lilien wrote for his English teacher at Stuyvesant High School and addressed to his schoolmates. It tells so much about Little Red and is so perceptive that De Lima says, "With Bob Lilien's permission we reprint this essay. Some of us felt that if we had had it earlier we need not have written this book" (1942, 217). He wrote, "Of course, there were our regular academic subjects. Arithmetic, *grammar*, spelling, and so on" (219, emphasis added).

"The trouble is," confesses an Agatha Christie character, "when you remember things, you don't always remember them right, do you?" (1972, 119). Our memories are not always accurate. But neither are the reports that on-the-spot witnesses give or the narratives historians construct. Our memories are not always consistent, either: in our interviews, we sometimes contradict each other and occasionally we even contradict ourselves. The thick book with the faded red cover that sat in my parents' black bookcase for forty years makes it possible to confirm—or for that matter, disconfirm—what we, the Little Red School House class of '43 remember decades after the fact.

Did our love of poetry really come about in the way my classmate recalled? In the De Lima book, it says:

> "No poetry, please" was one child's frank plea at the beginning of a reading period. However, before many weeks our poetry-reading period was one of the most popular of the day ... For weeks every poetry-reading period had to begin with or close with "The Congo." Many of the children learned the poem by heart and often found themselves reciting it, beating out the rhythm as they did so. By this time all opposition to poetry was dead. The very ones who had first objected were frequently asking for more and the poetry period was expanded to a full forty-five minutes, with the children calling for more time. Poems by Blake, Wordsworth, Sandburg, and many more became favorites. (1942, 93)

Of course the interviews contain more than remembrances of fifty years past. When a classmate says, "I don't understand what they do in the schools today. I really don't, but I know there is something wrong. The children don't enjoy education. They don't enjoy learning, and that's wrong because children are like sponges: they *love* to learn," she is speaking as her adult self—a present-day critic of our nation's schools. The ideas she expresses may have been influenced by her Little Red experience, but she is not seeing her school experiences as she did when she was a child. When, however, someone says, "We always made cookies, chopped up the fruits and citrus and put them in for the Christmas fairs we had here every year, and kids would, you know, try to eat it as they were chopping it up, and the first time I did it, after seeing everybody else and being very good, I put one in my mouth and Miss Beeman yanked me out and said 'Now you've got to stop that!' Oh, the injustice of it. I thought that was terrible," you can almost hear a schoolgirl's voice.

My classmates and I look back at Little Red from a much greater distance than did Bob Lilien. Yet when we talk about what happened in school—rather than what we now think about our school experiences or about American education today—our memories of Little Red are of a piece with his. Says one woman, "When I meet the classmates today, I don't see them as today, I see them as then. And I knew them *well*. I knew them *well*." When we talk about Little Red we often see it in the same way: we see it as then and we knew it well.

Sandy, who became a psychiatrist after twenty-five years as a pediatrician, might disagree that the interviews often come close to capturing and preserving the children's point of view. The summer after I notified classmates of the grant from the Spencer Foundation, he wrote me a perceptive letter in which he said: "One of Alfred Adler's neat observations was that adult first memories are highly selective, often poignant, distillations of the central issues of a particular childhood. Your study, timed as we experience half-price movies and patronizing hospital clerks, may well generate data that tell as much about our feeling for our current selves, as reflect on who and what made us this way."

The interviews may indeed reveal more about my classmates' adult lives than I realize, yet when I read them together with the De Lima book and take my own memories into account, the data converge. Moreover, every time I read through the interviews I think of what Kyoko Mori wrote in her memoir, *Polite Lies*:

> When we talk about the past with family, we often find that each of us remembers different aspects of the same experience. Though the difference in memory can sometimes lead to bickering, it's a relief to know that none of us has the sole responsibility for remembering—what we forget will be recalled by someone else. We occasionally learn details we didn't know because we were too young at the time or lived too far away. Family stories can shed a new light on the events we think we know. After the conversation, we add the new pieces to our memory. In this way, the past can expand rather than shrink. (1997, 32)

We the Little Red School House class of '43 are not literally family, yet I believe that the same holds true for us. Our memories fill in, correct, and amplify what each of us separately recalls.

Ah School, Ah Beautiful School

Some three-quarters of a century later, I have three sharp memories of my first day at Little Red: (i) Mr. Marvin sits me down next to three girls at what is either a table or four desks facing each other—I no longer remember which. "What's your name?" I ask the girl next to me. "Mary Jane," she replies. "What's yours?" I ask the girl opposite. "Mary Jane," she says. I am rendered speechless, but it turns out that she is telling the truth. I soon learn that we have two Mary Janes, two Joans, two Olgas, three—or was it four—Davids, and about twenty-five assorted others, including a Gier and a Gideon. (ii) At recess, I am standing alone in the playground. Every single girl in the class runs up to me, tells me her name, says she does or does not want to be my friend, and runs away. (iii) Only one boy speaks to me all day. He zooms up, points to the pickle-shaped pin on my coat lapel that I proudly acquired at the Heinz exhibit of the New York World's Fair, yells "pickle puss," and disappears.

In the film *Auntie Mame* progressive school children love to play at being a family of fish so that is what they do all day. In my favorite Josephine Tey mystery novel, *Brat Farrar*, a young woman calls the local progressive school "a school for dodgers" and says of it, "No one is forced to learn anything. Not even the multiplication table" (Tey 1950, 96) and a student at the school complains, "You can't imagine the screaming boredom of it. You simply can't imagine. There is nothing, but I mean *nothing*, that you are forbidden to do" (138). And then there is the joke a friend of mine likes to tell about the progressive school she went to in the 1930s: "When we got to school we used to say, 'Do we have to do whatever we want to do today?'"

In *The Transformation of the School*, Cremin calls the pedagogy Rousseau sets forth in *Emile* "laissez-faire" (1961, 103) and fifty years later a journalist attaches that same label to Miss Irwin's Little Red (Hampton, 27). One has only to read *Emile* and the De Lima book to know how wrong-headed this is.

My dictionary defines *laissez-faire* as "the theory that government should intervene as little as possible in the direction of economic affairs" (Stein 1980, 493). Although Rousseau strenuously opposed didacticism, his pedagogy was thoroughly interventionist. In *Emile* he says, "While the child is still without knowledge, there is time to prepare everything that comes near him in order that only suitable objects for him to see meet his first glances ... You will not be the child's master if you are not the master of all that surrounds him" (1979, 95). Then again: "Let him always believe that he is the master, and let it always be you who are. There is no subjection so perfect as that which keeps the appearance of freedom" (120). The examples Rousseau gives of his imaginary boy Emile's education match his words:

> Emile goes for a walk with his tutor Jean-Jacques. They get lost—or so Emile thinks—and Jean-Jacques' probing questions turn the walk into a geography lesson.

> On another walk Emile sees a stick in the water and with Jean-Jacques' probing questions Emile learns about refraction.

> Emile decides to plant a garden. Jean-Jacques gives a helping hand knowing full well that the plot belongs to a local farmer. The farmer whose melon patch Emile has unwittingly destroyed berates the boy. The farmer, Emile, and Jean-Jacques talk over the problem and Emile acquires the idea of private property.

As for Miss Irwin's supposedly laissez-faire pedagogy, here is my classmate Johnny's account of a typical day in the 10s. I reprint it from *Pen in Hand*, a collection of our writings:

Monday

> I come skipping into school. Ah, school, ah, beautiful school. Bang, crash, rip, slash, thud, I fall down the stairs of the coatroom. Some boys are kicking the socker ball around in the coatroom. I throw my coat up on the thing you hang your coat on, and come upstairs. Most everybody is playing stooping game. So what do I do? I go in. Clank, clank goes the piano. It stops; everybody throws themselves on the floor. The judge says, "John, you're out." Oh cuss, oh well, I can draw. Oh, oh, Marvin comes in! "Everybody take your seats and read, or I'll know the reason why, (or in other words, *or else.*)" I take out my book and read. At 9:30 Marvin says, "Everybody that wants to go to the library go," but I mostly don't because it seems like I always have a book when he says that. At 10:30 the ten-thirty music group goes off; I am in it. Then at 11 the eleven o'clock music group goes, and then we do arithmetic. At 11:30 we go to rhythms.

I think that's fun. Sometimes when we come back we do spelling. We have to study about twenty words, then he dictates them to us and we have to write them down. Then we go to lunch. Some people think the food there stinks, but I like the food there a lot. When we come back we go to shop. I am making a bookcase. Then at 2 o'clock we go to playground. I play socker; some of the group play dodge ball. At 3 o'clock we go home. Ah school, ah beautiful school.[4]

Johnny forgot to include our almost daily poetry periods in his Monday chronicle:

Has the teacher Bill Marvin come up in other people's talking about Little Red? He was very interested in poetry.

I remember learning a great deal of poetry. We actually memorized poetry, and I associate it with my second year there. Being ten and having a particular teacher ... a man who loved poetry. We read it aloud and we memorized it. I still remember bits and pieces of it.

I can remember another teacher named Mr. Marvin—that was in the Tens—and we would sing/chant Vachel Lindsay, a rhythmic poem, and we would clap our hands, and so on.

I have no words to convey the thrill of clapping our hands to the beat of "The Congo":

Boomlay, boomlay, boomlay, BOOM.
THEN I had religion, THEN I had a vision.
I could not turn from their revel in derision.
THEN I SAW THE CONGO, CREEPING THROUGH THE BLACK,
CUTTING THROUGH THE JUNGLE WITH A GOLDEN TRACK

or chanting along with Mr. Marvin sections of "Caliban in the Coal Mines," "The Highwayman," "The Ballad of the Harp-Weaver," "O Captain! My Captain!," "Tiger, Tiger," and all the other poems we came to know. School children used to be required to memorize poems. In the 10s no one told us to do so. We just did. We didn't have to work at it. We breathed Mr. Marvin's poems in with the air.

Johnny does not mention the ancient Hebrews and Egyptians, but when we are in the 10s our lives are intertwined with theirs. One classmate tells her interviewer: "You weren't there so I've got to tell you. For our curriculum, we started with Genesis in the Bible, then were guided through the more interesting parts, until we ended up in Egypt. And then that was one that we really concentrated on and ended up ... putting on a play and writing the music and all of that stuff."

We know the Egyptian pharaohs and their gods and empathize with the Hebrew slaves who have to make bricks without straw. To this day I can sing the refrain of the song our class composed for a dramatic production about the Hebrew slaves in Egypt:

> Down in the brickyards working all the day
> Lord come help us, lead us away.
> Oh Lord, come now, lead us away.

The school assembly at which my class demonstrates how you prepare a mummy remains one of the high points of my life. You cannot imagine how proud I was to be one of the people who wrapped up our mummy on stage—the mummy happened to be Johnny—and then lifted him on high and carried him away.

Here are two poems inspired by our study of the ancients and collected in *Pen in Hand*. "Asp" was composed by one of our Joans and "I Stand a Mighty Temple" by one of our Mary Janes:

Asp

> He struck the sacred asp,
> He hit it to the ground,
> He took it up and buried it,
> In the deep cold ground.

I Stand a Mighty Temple

> I, so great and old,
> Guarding secrets long forgotten,
> Standing forever in Egypt,
> Egypt is my home.
>
> Old and deserted I stand,
> Long ago forsaken.
> Gone my ancient glories,
> Passed away with the years.

> Dead, ye holy priests,
> Dead and buried in your graves,
> But know, oh holy worshippers,
> That I forever live.
>
> I stand, a mighty temple,
> A temple of mighty gods,
> Gods no longer worshipped,
> Gone as in the past.

My disintegrating copy of *Pen in Hand* also contains this short untitled poem by Andy:

> What good is it to work, work, work, all day long,
> To work in grit and grain, to tug and pull,
> And at lunch a slimy sandwich to fill an empty space.
> Tug and pull all day long, with dirt here and there.
> The same old slavery!

Skyscrapers and Indians

The telephone rings shortly after the New Year in 2012 and it is the Olga whom we call Kay Kay. I tell her that I am finally writing my book about progressive education, and in reading over the interviews I see that our class seems to have remembered Mr. Marvin best of all our teachers:

> One of my fond memories was Marvin ... And he's reading poems. I mean, my whole grade, I bet you to this day, Kay Kay, and me and other kids we could all recite "The Highwayman."

> And then the 10s was Marvin and I think, looking back, he was obviously magnificent.

> Well certainly, that course with Bill Marvin was totally memorable; you know both the writing of poetry and the reading of it. I just remember that very well, and I remember him very well.

"Ah," Kay Kay sighs. "Mrs. Hawkins was the one." I was not in the 6s—first grade—but my classmates report:

> In the Sixes you learned the little world around you here in the city, how the city worked, and you learned at that time—which I don't

think kids learn today—how a city works. You could translate that information as adults. When you went to some other city you'd know: well, they are to have this, they have to have that, I mean, that's how I looked at. Wherever I went, I knew that this is what they're going to ask, or if I need that, I know where to go.

We also studied about transportation, that is, we talked about the boats that bring things in, the trains that bring things in, the trucks that bring things in. Transportation. We visited all these places: the train yards, oh and also the buses, bus stations, the boat piers where the boats were tied up.

You learned to read maps. We learned to read maps! Well the map, you see, was this Manhattan map. That was the early stage. Yep, that was a simplified map, if you think about it. That was an eye opener.

The appendix to the De Lima book contains a transcript of a discussion my class has after Mrs. Hawkins takes them on a trip to the top of the Empire State Building. Mrs. Hawkins begins by asking someone to draw a picture of the water the class saw out the Empire State Building window. One girl calls the river the Hudson and Mrs. Hawkins says, "Think a minute. Where were we in the Empire State Building?" and then "Which side was the Hudson?" Several children figure out that they had been looking at the East River, not the Hudson, and from this item of knowledge the class works its way into placing the Hudson, the East, and the Harlem Rivers in their proper locations.

Once the geography gets straightened out, the subject turns to skyscrapers. "Did you see them in the country?" Mrs. Hawkins asks one child. "In Wisconsin?" she asks another. And so is launched a dialogue. I would call it "Socratic," but these are six-year-olds and the topic is not the nature of truth or justice. It is about why skyscrapers exist, how they are built, the need for architects and engineers, the materials that are used, and what is required to make the buildings livable.

The discussion continues a week later and in the interim my class has taken another trip. This time, says Mrs. Hawkins, we saw "a big, big building being constructed." Guided by her persistent questioning, my classmates review their firsthand knowledge of the materials used in skyscraper construction and of how the work proceeds. They then talk in some detail about how the glass for the windows is made. Next, Mrs. Hawkins says: "You saw those big steel girders going in the other day. If you were going to build your skyscraper, where would you get that steel?" "In a factory" is the answer one boy gives. "Tell us more about the factory: where might it be?" "New Jersey," another boy says, and she replies, "It could be. At any rate, would it be in Manhattan?" These six-year-olds know better. They know, too, that it will take boats to get the steel across the river and onto their island. "What does the factory make steel out of?" Mrs. Hawkins wonders. And the discussion progresses until she says, "I found a story this morning. It is all about what we have been discussing," and reads it to my class.

One of the aims of the radical school reform movement of the late 1960s and early 1970s was to take down the wall of separation between school and the "outside" world. Little Red did this when I was there. The title of one chapter in the De Lima book is "Our Classrooms Have No Walls" and in the chapter on the 13s—eighth grade—Mr. Studer asks how a thirteen-year-old's interest can be channeled "into more serious and genuine aspects of contemporary life." His answer: "We must tear down the walls of the classroom and bring the world to him. And we must take him out into the world" (De Lima 1942, 113):

> The field trips, taking us out into the world to see how people worked and what they worked at. A field trip could be something as simple as walking down to the corner and watching workmen at a manhole who were working with a jackhammer and building something under the infrastructure of the street.

> Well, we used to go on long walks. I mean I remember walking my legs off some of the time. I remember going down to see the tugboats and to talk to the tugboat Captain.

> Field trips were wonderful, and they were wonderful because they were integrated as part of the classroom learning experience also. There was preparation beforehand. There was analysis and further study afterwards.... We went everywhere in the community.... We went to the fire department, we went to the Fulton fish market in the middle of the night. As grade school kids we went everywhere.

We went on a field trip like every week in first grade, and that was around the neighborhood.... One of the ones that comes in my mind right away was going to a horse barn. I don't know if it was on Bleecker Street or one of the other streets. We did spend a lot of time on Bleecker Street, because there was so much going on there. I was amazed to see that in all the barns which I had seen before were one level for people and animals, and there was a hayloft up above.... The horses walked up these ramps and I was just like, oh wow. That's very vivid to me.

I can remember going to the sugar factory. And I can remember going to, I think it was a separate trip, would have been the cake-baking Nabisco, maybe. I can remember going on, I believe it was Burl Ives's houseboat.

We took trips to the garbage, you know, how you process garbage into the barges were they took them away in those days. To a sugar factory, which was wonderful. We got little samples, marvelous.... It seems to me we went to a paper mill or something—I remember learning how paper was made. We went to the Fulton Fish Market which was grand, and the idea there was to see that the fish came in on the boats, in those days right there on Fulton street. I can still see it. Actually, it was very smelly but it was grand. And they load the fish off and you know how they process it.... They were building the subways at that time, so we learned about sand bars, how tunnels were built.

The appendix to the De Lima book also contains an entry from Miss Stall's diary that is unmistakably about my class when we are in the 8s—third grade. The title of the chapter describing that year is "The Eights Are Indians," and my classmates wax eloquent over that year:

In the Eights you learned about Indians, and that was a whole new world. It was marvelous. You learned from the Indians: from soup to nuts, so to speak. You learned how they lived, how they made food, what they did, where they were, and all this sort of thing. You learned everything about them—the whole culture really. Plus, their music—so it was all incorporated.

Since we were studying Indians, we went to several museums and several places in Manhattan which were former Indian compounds. There are still a few marks that are in and around the city of New York.

Sewing buttons on Navajo costumes is a lifetime memory.

Well, with third grade being the study of the Indians, starting in the West and working our way East—I don't know. Now, at least particularly for me, I was just—it pushes a button in all sorts of ways for me right away.

I loved Dorothy Stall.... I remember we studied Indians, and I'm still interested in American Indians to this day. I remember the looms that we had hanging from the ceiling. I was very emotionally involved in that learning experience.

At a recent mini-reunion, my friends spoke about Miss Stall's 8s as if they could still see the pueblo the class built, the looms that hung from the ceiling, and the kachina dolls.

According to Miss Stall's diary, after my class goes on a walk through the Village along what once were Indian paths, she reads them a story about fishing in which the Indians pray to their net and thank the fish for allowing themselves to be caught. The story time spills into arithmetic. "The net was seven fathoms long, and another net they had was ten times that long, so we began a page in our arithmetic book called 'Measurements' and put in problems about fathoms and feet," she writes. And then she records for posterity how Phyllis, Paul, a Joan, and a Mary Jane use the kernels of Indian corn she distributes in order to solve the problem of how far an Indian runner travels each day if it takes him five days to carry a letter 180 miles.

William the Conqueror and a Printing Press

Remembering that in Miss Eastburn's 11s we learned about William the Conqueror, 1066, and the Battle of Hastings, I ask my husband, who went to a traditional public school in Cincinnati, Ohio, "What did you learn about the Middle Ages in elementary school?" He looks at me as if I have lost my mind and says, "Nothing." "Did you learn about 1066 and the Norman Conquest?" "No," he replies. "Did you learn about the serfs and the guilds?" His answer is "No." "Did you learn about the Black Death?" "No." "The invention of the printing press?" "No, I didn't even know what the Middle Ages was."

Thinking of what one of my classmates told her interviewer, I say to my husband, "Maybe you weren't listening when your teacher taught your class about the Middle Ages." As she recalls:

> My father came in sixth grade while we were discussing William the Conqueror and I was paying absolutely no attention, none. I had, I've forgotten what you call them … these things with sixteen squares and fifteen numbers that you can move around and line up; well, it happened to be his and I had lifted it out of his top drawer, and I was sitting playing with it, and I fell over backwards. And on the way home he said to me "Tell me about William the Conqueror," and I said "Who?"

"I have told you a thousand times," my husband says reprovingly, "that I was a very good child. It was very boring but I always paid attention in school."

In the 11s, we not only learn about serfs and guilds and the Norman Conquest. We sing the thirteenth-century Middle English song, "Sumer Is Icumen In":

> Sumer is icumen in,
> Lhude sing, cucu;
> Groweth sed
> And bloweth med,
> And springth the wode nu;
> Sing, cuccu!

We put on a play about the Black Death for which Kathy and I do the lights. Best of all, we learn to set type. "We had a print shop in the classroom and we were learning to set type. It was wonderful," one of us recalls. Another says: "The 11s was the Middle Ages, and we also learned about printing. We learned about books. We had our own printing press and we made our little book and wrote little things. That was important." The De Lima book contains a photograph of George and Moyra setting type. They appear to be hard at work, and I am willing to bet that this is the way they see themselves, for I remember setting type and feeling that same sense of responsibility about getting the job done correctly that I had when I was on stage wrapping up Johnny. You see, we were not learning to set type just for the fun of it. The printing press project grew out of our study of the late Middle Ages and Gutenberg's Bible.

In 1980 historian Elizabeth Eisenstein published *The Printing Press as an Agent of Change*, a two-volume work that gives Gutenberg's invention of the printing press the important place in history it deserves. Before that, textbooks tended to cite it in passing—as something that happened after the Black Death and before the discovery of America. For us in the 11s, Gutenberg's invention is already center stage. No one can say that we are reenacting Gutenberg's historic achievement. But in the 10s we got a feel for what it was like to write on papyrus, and in the 11s we discover how amazing it must have been to see words appear on the printed page.

We are not just typesetting arbitrary strings of words. We are printing a magazine filled with poems and stories written and edited by us. We call our magazine "The Composing Stick" and all these years later I can still make out the linoleum cut of a tree and the moon on the cover of my disintegrating copy. Down the left-hand side and across the bottom it says, "THE COMPOSING STICK" in large black stick letters and in smaller whitish lettering it reads, "WRITTEN, ILLUSTRATED, AND PRINTED BY THE 11'S OF LRSH." Phyllis and Moyra wrote the preface, Kathy and I were two of the printers, George and Moyra were two more, someone else—I think it was one of our Davids—did the cover, and almost every member of the class provided copy.

Here are three samples of our writing: "Poem" is by Joe, "A Pool" is by Judy, and "Shipyards" is by Paul:

Poem

White crust,
Lying on the open field.
Thin drifts,
Here and there.

Tufts of grass
Sticking though the crust.
The sharp, cutting
Wind blowing.

White crust,
Lying on the field.

A Pool

In the woods there's a pool
That is lovely and cool
So deep and green and dark.
And over it flies.
'Gainst the deep blue skies
A happy, singing lark.

Shipyards

Bang! Crash! Rat-a-ta-tat. Cranes screech, riveting hammers blast at the hull of a light cruiser on the way of a shipyard, any shipyard.

Pat Donovan, a grizzled old Irishman, yells at his helper "You blankety! Blank! Good for nothing farmhand! Where the HECK is that riveting hammer?"

Frank Pasatino yells back "Cant you see I'm lookin for it."

"No I couldn't say that I do."

"Why you blankety!"

"Oh yeah!"

This goes on and on. It is typical of the men. But without them we wouldn't be the country that we are. Bang! Crash! Rat-a-tat-tat.

In another part of the shipyard, an architect moans to himself, "Only 4 weeks ahead of schedule while number 13's cruiser is 7 months ahead.

Oh whad'll I say, oh dear me."

Bang! Crash! Rat-a-tat-tat! An enormous traveling crane swings a ten ton piece of armor plate into place.

Hey get her steady."

"What!"

BANG! CRASH! RAT-A-TAT-TAT! This is a shipyard.

Adverbs, The Triangular Trade, and the Bill of Rights

In the 12s—seventh grade—we play "In the Manner of the Word." We sit in a circle and our teacher Mr. Stevenson—or Steve, as we call him—picks one of us to be "It." The "It" person leaves the room and the rest of us choose an adverb—for instance, *happily*, *excitedly*, or *sleepily*. Whoever is "It" returns and commands someone to perform an action—for instance, sharpen a pencil or run around the room or tie a shoelace—in the manner of the word. The one who is "It" then tells another person to do something else, and so on. The "It" person may guess the word we have chosen in a flash or take forever to figure it out.

Even though my miming skills are minimal and we are not allowed to speak, I absolutely love this game. It is, by the way, the only one I remember playing at Little Red—not counting dodge ball and the other games we played when we went to the playground. We had spelling bees in Mr. Stevenson's class, and I can still hear my team's collective groan when I leave out one of the "m's" in "accommodate," but I am not sure that a spelling bee is a game. There was of course the stooping game of Johnny's "Monday": we skipped around the room, stooped down when the music stopped, and whoever dropped down last was out. But we did this each morning in the 10s before the school day began. I should know. I was the one clanking "Turkey in the Straw" on the piano.

In telling his interviewer "It was a wonderful education where on the one hand I never thought that they taught us anything and on the other hand I thought they taught us a great deal," one of my classmates has helped me understand why a naïve observer might accuse progressive education of being too laissez-faire. When we form our circle to play "In the Manner of the Word," we are not consciously trying to learn anything. From our standpoint—and perhaps also from the standpoint of a naïve observer—we are simply playing a game and having tremendous fun. From Mr. Stevenson's standpoint, however, this is a grammar lesson and we are learning about adverbs.

Although we were often unaware that when we were having a good time we were also learning, games played a small role in our life in school. In the letter in which Emily described Mrs. Landeck, she also wrote: "I remember particularly a study of the Triangular Trade in which Judy (not very well assisted by yours truly) and I drew a huge map on the floor of the classroom. Then we painted it and indicated how the Triangular Trade worked transporting sugar, rum and slaves ... While time has made things just a bit hazy, I probably could still give the gist of the Triangular Trade." I, too, can still give the gist of it, and I can also recite the First Amendment to the Constitution.

In my freshman year of college, an essay question on my Gov. 1 exam almost does me in. Neither the professor nor my section man has told us to memorize the First Amendment to the Constitution, and my previous schooling did not train me to make advance preparations of this sort. So, there I sit in a near catatonic state when a song Mrs. Landeck taught us pops into my mind. "Congress shall make no law," I hum as I open my bluebook and begin to write.

When I was young, children in New York City's public schools were singing "Morning is dawning and Peer Gynt is yawning" so as to be able to identify correctly the theme of Grieg's Peer Gynt Suite. Meanwhile at Little Red we were singing a song that begins "Congress shall make no law," continues through "the redress of grievances," and ends with a flourish that is halfway between a brass fanfare and a football cheer: "It's the Bill of Rights. It's the Bill of Rights. (Then faster and faster) It's the Bill of Rights, The Bill of Rights, The Bill of Rights, The Bill of Rights. (Then very slowly) The Bill of Rights!"

In May 2011, the *New York Times* reported that on a recent national civics exam fewer than half of American eighth graders knew the purpose of the Bill of Rights (Dillon 2011). We studied the Bill of Rights in some depth in the 12s, and perhaps also in the 13s, for I seem to associate our song with Miss Kneeland's class. But the 12s is the year we wrote and produced plays about Anne Hutchinson and John Peter Zenger. "I also remember being in a play that we did about Peter Zenger who was an early journalist from, I think, Rhode Island, and it was a freedom of the press issue," a classmate remembers.

You will find neither Hutchinson nor Zenger listed in that large compendium of "What Every American Needs to Know," *The Dictionary of Cultural Literacy*. Yet I take their absence to be a failing of *The Dictionary*, not a mark against our plays' protagonists. Zenger's libel trial in New York, not Rhode Island, in 1735 is one of the most important events in the history of journalism and is a landmark legal case in the development of freedom of the press in this country. Anne Hutchinson is right up there in importance with Roger Williams. Banished from the Massachusetts Bay Colony for teaching that an individual can communicate directly with God without the help of bible or ministers, she was one of this nation's first and most courageous exponents of religious tolerance.

"You were lucky," a reader of an early draft of this book tells me. "You were getting more conceptual things than I got until college. You were getting the meaning of the facts." The De Lima book confirms this impression. Once when another class of 11s was studying the earth's motion in relation to that of the sun and the planets, a girl said that she had learned all about this at her other school. De Lima reports: "She could not tell us about it, but she would read what she had in her notebook. She read five statements about the earth which were all true but which had no concrete reality for her or for her listeners. Asked if she could explain her notes so that we could understand them better, she said that she could not but that her teacher had told her that if she would repeat them over and over enough times she would know them." (De Lima 1942, 101)

Little Red did not want to turn out children who could recite facts at the drop of a hat but did not know the meaning behind them. Referring to her college experience, one classmate says: "I was a very good student and I graduated Phi Beta Kappa and I was in the history Honors Society and I knew that it was because I had learned to think conceptually at Little Red, that facts weren't just something to memorize but that there were reasons, and looking for the reasons and the connections enabled me to remember a whole bunch of stuff and that it wasn't that my intellect was so great but that I had used it correctly."

Floor, Door, Window, Ceiling

In September 1999 we have a reunion in Clinton, Connecticut. This is a landmark year for my class: we Depression babies are turning seventy. Kay Kay is the first to make the leap, but the rest of us are catching up and many of us are apprehensive about what the decade will bring. "What's wrong with being seventy?" asks our hostess. "Nothing's wrong," we reply and with rising spirits a group of us heads outside to gaze at the Long Island Sound and reminisce about Little Red.

"In her letter Emily mentioned 'Floor, door, window, ceiling.' Who here remembers that?" I ask when there is a lull in the conversation. "We do," say Kay Kay, one of our Joans, and Heather, and the four of us begin conducting 4/4 time per Mrs. Landeck's recipe. This gets Heather started on her stint in the school orchestra.

Judy's brother—he was four years younger than us—used to tune her violin for her. One day he was absent so Mr. Gold, the conductor, found Heather out. "Mr. Gold could have humiliated me," she says. "But you know what he did?" We all remember the silent man with the thick glasses who played the piano for Mrs. Landeck until he left Little Red to be a Hollywood composer. "He invited me to be his assistant conductor." "Imagine that," we murmur. "Who knew he could be so nice." When we go back inside, we congregate around the piano and Heather conducts the newly energized group of Depression babies in "Stenka Razin," "A Mighty Ship Was the Gundremar," "Casey Jones," and "Now Is the Month of Maying."

One month later, the Boston contingent of the Little Red School House class of '43 goes out to dinner in Cambridge. Over dessert Ann talks about the time she and another girl had a fight on the playground. Of course I remember. We all stood around and watched. What I now learn is that when we got back to our classroom Mr. Marvin took her aside and said, "You think you can do anything just because your mother is dead." "He should not have said that. The loss of a mother is too devastating for a young child," that reader of the early draft of this book told me. Ann herself says, "It was a risky thing to say to a 10-year-old but it worked. I never did anything like that again."[5]

That confession inspires Henry to tell us how Mr. Marvin changed his life. He says that whenever he felt an injustice had been done—mainly but not only to him—he blew up and got in a fight with the guilty party. One day on the way back from lunch, Mr. Marvin drew him to the back of the line for a talk. "I remember sitting on the curb and he asked me if I realized how often I blew up. He made me see that I shouldn't be getting in fights and I didn't get in another one the rest of the year. But then we went to June Camp."

Henry recalls a classmate's birthday at June Camp when we were in the 10s.

We were having a treasure hunt. There were lots of teams and mine was way ahead. So Allan told his team to follow mine and then they would find the clues. And I thought that was very unjust and I blew up and started to fight with Allan. He was my best friend and I had never fought with him but this wasn't right. And everyone stood around and watched us and then Marvin broke it up. He said he thought I had said I wouldn't blow up like that and I said, "But I only do it when I'm right." He said, "Look at all the others. They never do it. Don't you think they're sometimes right?" And I was so ashamed I left the group and climbed up a tree and stayed there the rest of the day. Finally I climbed down and went to my bunk and on my bed were lots of little pieces of paper, each one with some cake crumbs on it. And there was a note that said, "Henry. We noticed that you missed the party. So here is some cake for you." So, although I was mortified at what I had done, I was able to join the group again.

"Even the worst 'problem child,' so called, is a problem only part of the time," says De Lima. "Frequently also problems evaporate. The child outgrows the stage in which they occur, or deft handling on the part of a wise teacher or parent will help the difficulty to blow over" (1942, 10). Some of us remember being difficult in school. One woman tells her interviewer: "I was a difficult student. I was always getting into trouble ... I was on occasion or more often—I'd like to think more often than maybe it actually was—was removed from the classroom for misbehavior—I was very lively in school—and sent to the principal's office.... And that was Miss Irwin. I remember her office. There was a huge wall full of books and I think there was a couch, and it was a pleasure to be sent to her office. I remember it very fondly." Another recalls "being one of the disrupters of class and spending a fair amount of time sitting out in the hall because I wouldn't shut up."

On two occasions our class as a whole appears to have "acted out." One of us recalls Mr. Marvin's deft handling of a water pistol situation: "For a while we all brought water pistols to school. Mr. Marvin got tired of it. You know, we'd sit there going [she made gestures]. I mean, we were naughty in a sense. We pushed the limits.... And so he required us to bring water pistols one day, and raincoats, and we all went up on the roof and we shot each other for an hour and he said, 'Now, I never want to see another water pistol in the school, and he didn't.'"

Others remember Miss Harris's skillful handling of The Strike in the 9s—fourth grade. Miss Harris is the one teacher my classmates do not remember kindly:

> She was mean.... She was a mean lady. I mean the people in the class felt she was mean too, at least I think they did.

> I acted out quite a bit in her class. I don't remember acting out in Miss Stall's class at all.

> We didn't like Harris very much. She was not as sweet a heart as Mabel Hawkins.... We had her twice, when we were seven and then when we were nine in-between was Dorothy Stall for the eights, but I know that we certainly were not happy that we were getting her [Miss Harris] back at nine.

> In fourth grade we had a teacher named Miss Harris. How she happened to be plunked down in the middle of a progressive school I don't know because Miss Harris was extremely strict and I didn't like Miss Harris.... My father pointed out to me that in adulthood I would look back on her as an excellent teacher and my father was right.

In light of these sentiments, one can see why The Strike occurred in Miss Harris's 9s not Miss Stall's 8s or Mr. Marvin's 10s:

> When people get my hackles up, even when I was a kid, I tend to get very rebellious, and I led this big strike against rest hour in her class. Of course she found me out. I had written a note that said "Down with rest hour" and we're going up the stairs, the stairway at Little Red. And I don't know, the note fell out of my hand or somebody's hand and right at her feet, and it was a lot of trouble.

> There was a round of strikes in 1936, the United Auto Workers, the sit-down strike was invented and we heard about it on the radio, saw pictures on the front of the paper of workers sitting and heard our parents talk about it, so we had to have our strike and we held our strike and that was a big event. As far as I can remember, and I've thought about this ... I don't think we had any demands, we just had a strike.

I never knew Miss Harris but my classmates' memories of The Strike have me convinced that she dealt with it brilliantly:

> When I look back on it I say Harris handled it so neatly. She said, "Well, are you going to have a strike? Well, okay, don't you need to have a strike committee?" "Well yes, we've got, we did have to have a strike committee," and, "Would you like to have a secret meeting with the strike committee?" "Oh, yes, we would like to have that." And as I remember, the strike committee, it ended up being the whole class, and we were given a separate room, and Miss Harris let us go in there to have our meeting and we had our meeting. And I think probably, I don't remember well, but at a certain point she came in and said, "Well, okay, is the meeting over now?" "Well, yes," we guess it was. "Well, now you can come back in here and we'll go back to school."

> The class was debating about going on strike. I absolutely forget why we were doing this. And the strike was, in a sense was against some of the teachers or against some of the—it was sort of supervised by the teachers also I mean it was really a good thing from the gestalt. And I decided it was stupid. I wasn't going to do it.... And so I was brought before Miss Irwin and I was told in no uncertain terms that when the [people] go through a strike, you go on strike. Well, at that time, I was very unhappy about it.

Our teachers were not punitive. The school did not even keep children back. As one of my classmates explains, "We were kept together by age, not by achievement, so that we were on a par, in one way, always." Nor did we have the concept of an A, B, C, D, or F student. One man says in his interview that our parents informed us how well we were doing, and he draws from this the conclusion that "things were graded." I remember that we frequently took standardized tests and have the vague recollection that my parents told me my scores, but I do not otherwise recall ever thinking about or being told how I was doing in school. Says De Lima: "We send home no written reports. We give no marks, no gold stars, and we award no prizes. We give tests only to determine if the children are up to standard requirements" (1942, 9). And my classmates say:

> We never got put down. I don't remember being put down. We didn't get grades. We had nothing to be ashamed of. We never had

to go home with a D, you know. And, you know, we didn't have to go through those things.

It was unlike other schools I had been in.... Yes, it was fun in the sense that there was never any pressure applied, so that going to school was not ever associated with any sort of dread or any kind of fear.

I think one of the greatest achievements was to be able to get away with not testing. Eventually, you need it somehow, but you don't need it for the kids.... I'd say yes it's a school with—[it] did not press us or punish us or anything to do with that. You kind of learned because you felt you should and you wanted to, certainly.

No grades, no prizes, no awards, no gold stars, no dunce caps! "I knew a man in Scarsdale who had been, I think, the class behind me," says my classmate. "He felt that Little Red never taught him to compete in a world that is totally competitive, and you know, he was very angry about that." Miss Irwin believed that awards and competition are bad for children, and I tend to agree that for young children a little competition goes a long way. One summer my husband and I participated in a carpool. Our job was simple. He drove our two sons and two neighbor children to their day camp each Friday morning, and I drove them home each Friday afternoon. Well, Friday afternoon was when awards were handed out. The result: Four young children. Eight Fridays. Not a single prize among them. Back home we five would ride each week in grim silence.

Does Miss Irwin's philosophy mean that we were mollycoddled? In 1899, the very year that Dewey gave the lectures to parents that became *The School and Society*, the great philosopher and psychologist William James told teachers: "We have of late been hearing much of the philosophy of tenderness in education.... Soft pedagogics have taken place of the old steep and rocky path to learning." Equating tenderness with a smoothing away of difficulties, James objected: "The fighting impulse must often be appealed to. Make the pupil feel ashamed of being scared of fractions, of being 'downed' by the law of falling bodies, rouse his pugnacity and pride, and he will rush at the difficult places with a sort of inner wrath at himself that is one of his best moral faculties. A victory scored under such conditions becomes a turning-point and crisis of his character" (James 1958, 51–52).

Shame, wrath, and pugnacity did not figure in Little Red's conception of learning, but this does not mean that Mrs. Hawkins, Miss Stall, Miss Harris, Mr. Marvin, and the others pampered us. Mr. Marvin, the teacher I remember best, was a no-nonsense sort of person—not as strict as Miss Kneeland and with a more magnetic personality, but cut from the same cloth. Unbeknownst to me, my mother complained to him one parents' night about my having cut my wrist climbing over the playground fence. Had I dreamed she would do this, I would have protested loudly. The only reason I know this happened is that the next morning Mr. Marvin told me to my great embarrassment—actually to my mortification—that my mother was overprotective.

I like to think that at least a few teachers in James's audiences were aware that in proffering a warlike conception of learning as the only legitimate alternative to a pedagogy of tenderness, he was embracing an untenable dualism. Teachers do not have just those two choices. At Little Red we learned in large part because we engaged in activities and projects that we enjoyed and needed to see through to completion, and also because of our group responsibilities. "By six," says De Lima, "children can collect their own materials and supplies. They can help arrange the clay table. They can bring wood from the wood box and paper, crayons, and paints from the shelves; get their paint water and empty it; wash their easels and brushes and at the end of the period put things away. Usually a daily committee is appointed to clean up and sweep the floor" (1942, 46).

Did the absence of grades, gold stars, and the rest mean that we got away with murder and were allowed to believe that $7 \times 8 = 25$ or that the Battle of Hastings was in 1607? As one classmates says: "If something was correct, it was correct, but if it was wrong then you were explained as to why it was wrong. Not just that it was just wrong, but you got a reason, a rationale. And then you had to go back and think it through: now, how you would do it differently? In other words, I'm not going to sit here giving you the answer, but how would you do it differently?"

"As you know," says the person who told her interviewer that we had nothing to be ashamed of, "We were a million times encouraged." Says De Lima: "We believed in the beginning as we still do, that children can be happy in school ... and that life does not begin when school ends but rather, as John Dewey says, that *school is life*" (1942, 5, emphasis in the original).

Notes

1. 2000 or so a year according to De Lima (1942, p. 201).

2. The one book I know of that tells it like it was from the standpoint of the children is *Were We Guinea Pigs?* written by members of by the Ohio State University High School class of 1938.

3. If our school had had two or more classrooms per grade—if, for example, some of us had been in 5A, 6A, 7A, etc. and some in 5B, 6B, 7B—two of us might have studied grammar and the other three might not have. But at Little Red there was a single classroom for each grade level. If some of us had skipped grades, those children might in the process have missed out on the school's grammar teaching. At Little Red, however, children of the same age were placed together from the start and with very few exceptions, we stayed with our age group for as long as we remained in the school. If Little Red had resembled Summerhill—a progressive school in England that gave children the freedom to choose what they studied—it would have been possible that some of us were taught grammar and some of us were not. Our teachers explicitly rejected this laissez-faire philosophy, however. Similarly, if our school had instituted a system of individualized instruction such as the Dalton Plan, the wildly discrepant recollections about grammar could all be true. But although the teachers at Little Red knew each one of us very well and treated us as individuals, they did not design a special course of study for each child. The curriculum they planned was for the whole class.

4. The appendix in De Lima (1942) includes the schedule for each class.

5. The quotations from this dinner and from other reunions are taken from the notes I jotted down immediately after.

2 Child-Friendly Schools

Why Were We There?

George Orwell once wrote, "No one can look back on his schooldays and say with truth that they were altogether unhappy" (1984, 433). Until I read my classmates' interviews I had no idea how they felt about Little Red:

> I never understood the common mythology that kids hate school. I don't think we hated school—no, we *loved* school.

> What we were ashamed of is if we were late to school too often and we were sent home. This was a bad punishment, that we couldn't come to school that day.

> The school was actually a life-saving experience. "Life-saving" so that you didn't mess up your life. I always felt it was like a learning experience, continually. I mean, you know, you'd always learn something new. It was fascinating. To me, it was fascinating. I hated to miss it.

> You always felt cared for. You felt safe. Probably feeling safe was important to me. My early childhood didn't feel safe. And school became the place that was. And it was good.

> I simply loved everything about it.

> I mean it made me what I am.

> I adored school.... It was my life.

In the De Lima book, Miss Irwin and our teachers say, "What we most earnestly seek to do is to provide our children with a good life" (1942, 6) and the interviews convince me that they succeeded. I do not mean that every single one of us was happy at school every minute of every day. I think it fair to say that most of us led good lives in school most of the time.

Whether leading a good life in school was the reason our parents sent us to Little Red I cannot say. Ours was not a generation whose parents routinely sought their children's opinion before making decisions, and a number of my classmates appeared surprised when they were asked in their interviews why their parents had chosen Little Red. How should they know?

Of those who lived in Greenwich Village, some seemed to be under the impression that they were sent to Little Red because, like Mount Everest, it was there: "It was just sort of assumed that that was where I would go since we lived in the Village." Others thought their parents liked what they had read or heard about the school:

> I had been in a nursery school on East 19th Street and I think that—this is all hearsay because this is from my mother—I think that the teachers that were in that nursery school knew about the Little Red School House.

> My mother and father both knew about it and were both anxious, eager actually, to have us come to Little Red.... They were just avant-garde people, you know, and intelligent, and agreed with what they had read about it, I guess.

> [My mother] had read in the *New York Times*.... So, after she finished reading the article, she said it sounded like a school she could be interested in so she called Elisabeth Irwin and she was invited down for an interview. So, after the interview, I don't know how much later, I was accepted and I started.

One woman reported that her mother sent her two girls to the Little Red School House because "she wanted to prove to the other side [of the family] that her children were having a superior education." A man said, "In retrospect I am very surprised that my parents sent me there, because they were very conventional and very conservative." Someone else hazarded the guess that her "single working mother ... needed a school that took us as long as possible." And according to another: "One important consideration for my mother was that they gave the children a hot lunch and made sure they ate the lunch, because my mother always felt that I didn't eat enough and I was too little and skinny and wouldn't eat as much as she wanted me to. So at least that meant that someone else would get one meal a day into me."

I have only recently pieced together my own history. The year I entered Little Red, I began spending my Saturday mornings at a music school. I had been taking piano lessons since I was five but these theory and ear training classes were a brand-new experience. My music teachers were the very thorough, very straitlaced Mrs. Harris and the widely feared Miss Goldstein. After a concert I attended in Rockport, Massachusetts, in 2014, members of the audience had an opportunity to speak to the soloist. Having read in the program that Garrick Ohlsson had attended the very same music school as I, albeit some twenty years later, I ventured to ask him if he had had Miss Goldstein. "Yes," he replied enthusiastically. "She wore black," said I. "She smoked incessantly. She always had a cigarette in her hand," said he. "Strict," I ventured. "She was an excellent teacher," replied one of the great pianists of our time.

Miss Goldstein had a habit of referring to herself in the third person—as in, "Miss Goldstein does not like people who have not done their homework"—so that it was weeks before I realized that the woman in the black dress who was standing at the blackboard and address-ing the class was not a substitute teacher but Miss Goldstein herself. Mrs. Harris is the one, however, who said to my mother: "I don't know what to make of Jane. She never looks at me but when I ask her a ques-tion she always knows the answer." To my amazement my mother told Mrs. Harris that the reason I did not look at her during class is that I went to a progressive school. Then gazing into my eyes she whispered, "Oh, Janie, why can't you do what I used to do? Look at the teacher and think of something nice."

Historically, the progressive education of the early twentieth century represented a reaction to the traditional schooling my mother and her sis-ters were exposed to in New York City's public schools: desks bolted to the floor, children sitting quietly in rows with all eyes on the teacher, and days devoted to drill and rote learning. Says Charlotte Bronte's Jane Eyre when she first meets her future friend Helen: "I observed you in your class this morning, and saw you were closely attentive." Says Helen: "When I should be listening to Miss Scatcherd, and collecting all the things she says with assiduity, often I lose the very sound of her voice; I fall into a sort of dream. Sometimes I think I am in Northumberland, and that the noises I hear around me are a bubbling brook, which runs through Deepden near our house" (1997, 56–57).

Says one of my classmates of the school she attended before Little Red: "I remember the school quite well, I mean, the classroom anyway, as well. Children sat in rows and the teacher had a desk up in the front and all the children were very quiet and listened to the teacher, and I didn't fit in for that measure. I spent most of the time in the hall I think." Another compares Little Red with the school he had previously attended: "It was a change from the desks bolted in rows on the floor."

My mother, a teacher in the New York City public school system, wanted a better school for her one and only child than those she had attended and the ones she taught in. My father—"an old-time newspaperman" is how he described himself—did not go to school. He grew up on a farm in New Jersey in the arms of an extended immigrant family that was not his own and was tutored alongside the other children by Charles, the bachelor uncle. When I was young, my father talked endlessly about Charles. The things I remember best are: (1) Charles taught my father and the other young boy on the farm arithmetic by having them climb the cherry trees, pick the fruit, and sell it at the roadside; (2) at age nine my father single-handedly published a newspaper that he sold to passersby; and (3) Charles only owned one suit.

Shortly after my father died, I dined with a family friend whose mother grew up on that farm. I had recently written a scholarly paper about Rousseau's *Emile* and here finally was someone who would appreciate what I had discovered. Charles, I told her excitedly, was putting Rousseau's pedagogy into practice. "No," she said as if she had thought about this all her life, "it was Tolstoy." I had to agree. After all, Charles grew up in Russia and sported a Tolstoy-like beard. But on the basis of the "Tolstoy and Dostoyevsky" course I took in college, I was willing to bet that Tolstoy had read his Rousseau. Only while writing this book have I checked out my hunch. As it turns out, Tolstoy was Rousseau's disciple: he wore a Rousseau medallion around his neck, read all the master's works, especially admired *Emile*, and set up schools on his estate for the peasants based on Rousseau's pedagogy (Knapp 2004).

With a heritage like this, is it any wonder my father wanted me to go to a progressive school? The philosopher with the greatest influence on the kind of progressive education we had at Little Red was Dewey, not Rousseau. But all one has to do is read Dewey's *Schools of To-morrow* to know that he too was Rousseau's direct descendent.

I remember very little about the first progressive school I attended other than that it allowed me to go through reading and arithmetic workbooks at my own pace and that we made cameras out of shoeboxes. I think I liked it well enough but it was very small, and when two of the three other girls in my class became obsessed with clothes, my parents began their search for another school. They never told me why they ultimately chose one that was a long subway trip away from our apartment building. I suspect that one day on his way to work my father stopped in to take a look at Little Red, met Miss Irwin, and that was that:

I adored her. I thought she was incredible.

Elisabeth Irwin was so dear to me. I think we all loved her. There was something very charismatic about this woman.

We were all aware of her presence. Everybody totally loved her. And one of the things which helps create this kind of bonding that we had with her ... was that we had get-togethers every morning in what was then our auditorium. And we had music and she always read poetry to us and talked.

In his article for the parents' *Bulletin*, my father wrote of the 196 Bleecker Street building: "I like it. I get the sense Mark Twain would have been at home in it, would have claimed it for his own. Tom Sawyer and Huck Finn wouldn't play hookey from this school." Miss Irwin's "jovial spirit pervaded the whole place," wrote Mrs. Hawkins on the fortieth anniversary of the school's opening at Bleecker Street:

She had a wonderful sense of humor, accompanied by a twinkle in her eyes. She felt there should be fun associated with everything done in the school; yet she was a woman with serious thoughts, too. She always had time for children and parents and teachers; her door was always open. She wanted children to have plenty of time for growth. It was dead wrong, she felt, to have a child pushed into something before he was ready. But she held the faith that every child could be a great adult.

She had a very clear and simple way of expressing herself. Her remarks were always to the point and incisive. She had the rare ability to size up a situation and pass her good, down-to-earth judgment in remarkably short order and with the most picturesque language. You bet people listened! She solved problems rapidly, with a minimum of stress and strain. She was a fervent believer in truth and hated sham and hypocrisy.

Miss Irwin died of cancer in 1942. I don't think any of us children even knew she was ill. I have only one vivid memory of that time. Mrs. Landeck is standing at the door of our classroom and calls three or maybe four of us out into the hall. We follow her to the music room where people from other classes have already assembled. She hands this small, makeshift chorus the words and music of the two songs she wants us to sing at Miss Irwin's memorial service. The melody of the one I remember is from Brahms Academic Overture. Instead of "Gaudeamus igatur" we sing:

> We thy children hail thee, hail thee
> Our beloved leader.
> We thy children hail thee, hail thee
> Mother of our youth.

Fitting the School to the Child

Whenever an untraditional school is singled out as being really terrific, someone inevitably attributes its success to a charismatic leader who cannot be replaced. I saw this happen at a Harvard University symposium. Deborah Meier gave an impassioned talk about Central Park East, the school she founded in New York City, and when she was done the other speakers said, "Debbie, your school is a great success because you are a genius. But people like you can't be replicated. So, let's talk about what the average principal can do in the average school."

There can never be another Elisabeth Irwin or, for that matter, another Caroline Pratt, the founder of New York City's City and Country School; Carmelita Hinton, the founder of the Putney School in Vermont; Katharine Taylor, the inspired director of the Shady Hill School in Cambridge, Massachusetts; Marietta Johnson, the founder of the Organic School of Education in Fairhope, Alabama; Carleton Washburne, the superintendent of schools in Winnetka, Illinois; or William Wirt, the superintendent of schools in Gary, Indiana. Yet, I see no reason why the ideas these women and men put into practice cannot be passed down from one generation to the next as living legacies *if they are properly understood and the public so desires.*

In *The Transformation of the School*, Cremin calls progressive education "the educational phase of progressivism" (1961, viii) and Elisabeth Irwin came of age at the height of the Progressive Era. The kind of progressive education she instituted at Little Red might equally well be called the educational "expression" of progressivism. The members of this quintessentially American movement included two US Presidents—Theodore Roosevelt and Woodrow Wilson; several congressmen; Supreme Court Justice Louis Brandeis; muckraking journalists like Lincoln Steffens, Jacob Riis, Ida Tarbell, and Upton Sinclair; social reformers like Jane Addams, the founder of Hull House and a Nobel Peace Prize winner; Susan B. Anthony and numerous other feminist leaders; and the philosophers William James and our own John Dewey.

Some Progressives were rich, some were poor. Some were Democrats and some Republicans. What they shared was a belief in the "gospel of democracy" (Moyers 2004, 11) and a desire to improve the lives of all people in this country. Miss Irwin held the same convictions. By training a psychologist and by inclination a feminist who fought for women's rights and whose friend Jeannette Rankin was the first woman to be elected to Congress, she became an advocate for children. Our growth and development into people who care about those less fortunate than themselves and treasure democracy as a way of life is what Little Red was all about.

Today, as in my childhood, most educators assume that children must fit into the schools in which they are put. When they do not it is presumed to be their fault, their parents' fault, or else the fault of their teachers, their principals, or the school superintendent. Few ever seem to think, as Miss Irwin did, that there might be something fundamentally wrong with the very idea of tailoring children so that they will fit into school. Scarcely anyone seems to think, as she did, that school should be designed to fit the children it is supposed to educate.

In the 1920s, Miss Irwin wrote a book called *Fitting the School to the Child*.[1] This is what she was attempting to do in the experimental classes she established within the New York City public school system. When during the Great Depression the city stopped funding those classes and Little Red was founded, it is what she continued to do at 196 Bleecker Street.

At our August 2014 minireunion, Phyllis's husband who was in the class two years ahead of us described his first day at Little Red. Peter arrived in New York from England in the summer of 1939 and entered Miss Kneeland's 12s the very day I started in Mr. Marvin's 10s. "I had an English accent and wore a blue blazer and shorts," he informs us and we roll our eyes thinking about how this outfit must have struck his American classmates. "You remember the Houston Street playground? Well, Miss Kneeland suggested to the class that today for a change they play soccer not softball. I stood there all by myself and was of course the last one chosen for a team and my captain of course made me goalie. No one knew that I had been playing soccer all my life. So, when the ball came to me I caught it and kicked it all the way across the playground. That is how Miss Kneeland integrated me into the 12s."

Do you remember Henry's tale about not being able to read until age nine? In the United States today, children are being taught to read in kindergarten,[2] whereas formal reading instruction did not begin at Little Red until the 7s—second grade. If this seems much too old to you, be advised that seven is the very age it now starts in Finland whose school system is so heralded.

To my utter astonishment, one classmate of mine took that starting age literally:

> I remember that on my seventh birthday, I asked if I could go and see Elisabeth and was told, yes I could. So, I went down there and Mrs. Van what's her name said okay, and I went in to see her [Miss Irwin] and she said, what brings you here and so forth. And I said I'm seven today. She said, oh, happy birthday. And I said aren't I supposed to start at seven? She said well you don't have to. Did you want to? I said, yes, sure. So, she got out Dick and Jane, and we want through Dick and Jane. Yes, Elisabeth and I. We went through the whole pre-primer and everything and I said, thank you ... and she said goodbye and that was it.

By delaying reading instruction, we "eliminate automatically a whole host of difficulties due to the child's physical and intellectual insecurity," wrote De Lima (1942, 136). Furthermore, Miss Irwin told parents not to panic if their child could not read at age seven or eight or even nine, and the school itself did not take fright if it took some of us more than a year to develop this skill:

> It was not a major thing at Little Red to be able to read at age six. If it happened at seven or eight, it was fine, although it did shake up some parents!

> I was a slow learner. I don't think I really got down to reading 'til I was about seven or eight.

A woman in my class reports that when she left Little Red in the middle of the 8s for health-related reasons, she did not know how to read: "My mother kept trying to teach me to read. And by the time I was eleven, I was reading. I had difficulty learning to read. I was one of those children that had trouble learning to read." A man who describes himself as being dyslexic and in a special reading group recalls learning to read "probably in third or fourth [grade]. I got to the point where given the time, I could figure out what something says. I still read incredibly slowly." Another woman says,

> I was a kind of halting, not very good reader, and I remember I used to have to go to some kind of little spelling remedial—I mean in the little room, I remember being in a little room in Little Red with a few kids and a teacher trying to teach me how to spell *cherry* which I had a lot of trouble with. But in the 10s all the girls started to go crazy reading the Nancy Drew mystery stories, and I was not a good reader at that time, but I started, I had to be with everybody else, I started reading them. By the time I had read every single Nancy Drew book I was a fine reader.

Before Henry was born, Miss Irwin wrote: "It is within my recent experience to find a boy who when he was almost eight could not read the simplest primer and one year later was reading *Huckleberry Finn* with vast enjoyment and appreciation" (De Lima 1942, 55). And here is the learning-to-read story one of our Joan's told me many years ago.

It is the summer before the 7s and Joan is on vacation with her parents in Gayhead on Martha's Vineyard. On Sunday, they take her to the local Sunday school. The Gayhead Indian children are sitting in a circle and Joan happily joins them. My guess is that she is expecting an interesting discussion of the sort her class has recently had with Mrs. Hawkins. Instead, the Sunday school teacher hands the Bible—a real Bible, not a child's version—to one person in the circle and points to a passage. This five- or six-year-old reads the passage aloud and passes the Good Book on to the next child in the circle. And so it goes around the room with everyone there reading a passage aloud—that is, everyone but Joan. And everyone can see that Joan who is obviously one of the oldest children in the room DOES NOT KNOW HOW TO READ. Needless to say, when Little Red starts up in September Joan is ready and willing to learn. And she does.

Fitting the school to the child did not mean sitting back in laissez-faire fashion and waiting for the lightning to strike. It meant creating a child-friendly environment in which the urge to read would develop. In the De Lima volume, Miss Irwin wrote:

> If a child's day is filled with many varied interests and activities during his first years at school; if he begins to feel that he is master of the material world, that he can see the way to feed and clothe himself, that he can organize a group and put through a project; if he knows that information to help him further these ends is stored in books, he is not going to need artificial stimulation to learn to use them. When the moment comes to help such children to read a surprisingly short time is needed to establish them as better readers than their brothers early drilled by traditional methods. (1942, 54–55)

Learning without Drudgery

When one of my sons was in the sixth grade, he arrived home one afternoon with the news that the principal of his Massachusetts public school had walked into his classroom and said, "You children should not be chewing gum. Your parents don't chew gum when they go to their offices. School is your workplace and gum chewing is not allowed." So far as I know he was not a gum chewer. He simply disapproved of the comparison. "I don't like the idea that school is our workplace, do you?" he asked me.

Learning is the work that children do in the widely accepted "school as workplace" scenario. Hence the term "*work*sheets" for the pieces of paper with problems for them to solve in school. Hence the term "home*work*" for the tasks they are told to do at home. Hence assurance to those who do poorly on tests that if they *work* harder they will do better next time. And hence a journalist's approval in 2013 of the vision of school as "a learning factory" (Ripley 2013, 195).

An underlying assumption of the school-as-workplace way of thinking is that work is the opposite of play: work is difficult and play is easy, work is tedious and play is fun, work is serious business and play is frivolous. Why does the very thought of children playing and having fun in school horrify so many? The presumption is that they are frittering their time away and therefore they cannot possibly be learning anything of value.

Miss Irwin and our teachers did not share this joyless vision. Little Red was able to make good on its promise to give us a good life because, like Rousseau, it refused to divorce work from play. In describing the ideal education he would give the boy Emile, Rousseau said: "Whether he is busy or playing, it is all the same to him. His games are his business, and he is aware of no difference" (1979, 161). We at Little Red were aware of no difference, either.

To produce "The Composing Stick," our class has to write the poems and compositions that will fill it up and then do the necessary editing. We also have to learn to set type, do the type setting, choose a name for the magazine, design the cover, do the actual printing, and assemble the pages. In the process, we work very hard but it is not drudgery. We have a wonderful time printing and publishing our very own magazine. What I do not realize when I am an eleven-year-old is that the printing project at which we are at work is, from Miss Eastburn's point of view, a vehicle for teaching us those academic skills known as grammar, punctuation, spelling, and handwriting.

Little Red was not the only progressive school to reject the work/play dichotomy. A friend who attended the Francis Parker School in Chicago in the 1930s remembered writing a book about the history of Chicago with her third-grade classmates and the man who told me that school was his life recalls building the city of Ur in a sandbox. At both the Francis Parker School and the Shady Hill School, fourth graders studied the Greeks. Here is Evelyn Dewey's description of the Francis W. Parker's Greek experience:

> The work includes the making of a Greek house, and writing poems about some Greek myth. The children make Greek costumes and

wear them every day in the classroom. To quote Miss Hall, who teaches this grade: 'They play sculptor and make clay statuettes of their favorite gods and mould figures to illustrate a story. They model Mycenae in sand-pans, ruin it, cover it, and become the excavators who bring its treasures to light again. They write prayers to Dionysius and stories such as they think Orpheus might have sung. They play Greek games and wear Greek costumes, and are continually acting out stories or incidents which please them. To-day as heroes of Troy, they have a battle at recess time with wooden swords and barrel covers. In class time, with prayers and dances and extempore song, they hold a Dionysiac festival. Again, half of them are Athenians and half of them Spartans in a war of words as to which city is more to be desired. Or they are freemen of Athens, replying spiritedly to the haughty Persian message.' ... the work so becomes a part of their lives that it is remembered, as any personal experience is retained, not as texts are committed to memory to be recited upon. (1915, 124–5)

Historian Eugene Provenzo reports that the progressive practices of the Park School in Buffalo instituted by Mary Hammett Lewis in 1912 remained a vital part of the school's culture well into the 1960s when he attended. "Take the cider making," he writes, "I remember that our cider was brown and sugary—nothing like the thin cider at the grocery store. We had the pleasure of selling it and making a little money for school projects. We also made the extraordinary discovery that when left to age, our cider would ferment and become effervescent and mildly alcoholic. We wrote about making and selling the cider, and of course, we had to keep records of our business venture and calculate our profits. The learning came naturally" (1999, 110).

Eunice Jones, a teacher at the progressive school established at Arthurdale, a New Deal resettlement for impoverished families from the coal camps of West Virginia, wrote in her diary that her

second graders built a replica of the Arthurdale village with scrap lumber they collected throughout the project. As they located building materials, the second graders witnessed the actual construction of their community and planned in detail how their own construction was to take place. Children observed the use of various tools; they learned to use a level and a square in carpentry and a guide line in laying out stone masonry. In constructing their village, they learned such mathematical concepts as the relation of a part to a whole, equivalents, measures and measuring, and fractions. They also learned to cooperate and communicate, as they developed a common interest by working toward a shared end, broadening and enriching horizons that had been severely limited by life in the idle coal camps. (Perlstein and Stack 1999, 220)

The second graders, Jones recorded in her diary, "were so delighted" with their construction project that as they wrote a story about their village "they laughed and laughed" (Perlstein and Stack 1999, 220).

At the very time my classmates and I were putting on plays about Anne Hutchinson and John Peter Zenger, my friend Pat and her sixth grade classmates at the Lincoln School in New York City were studying Latin America. A booklet Agnes De Lima wrote with the teachers of the two Lincoln School sixth-grade classes describes the children's use of the resources in the school library; their museum trips to learn about the Mayan, Aztec, and Inca cultures; a visit to a Latin American print exhibit; the films they saw; and the assembly program they presented to the entire school. It also contains photographs of the children concentrating on what they are doing: in this case, constructing maps, painting murals, making clay figures and pottery, and broadcasting to South America (De Lima, Tompsie, and Francis 1942).

The Josephine Tey character who calls the local progressive school "a school for dodgers" and says that anyone can go there "who loathes hard work and has a parent with enough money to pay the fees" (Tey 1950, 96, 138) takes the wedded union of school and work for granted. The notion that children in progressive schools spend their days at play having fun and not learning fits Tey's caricature of us as spoiled rich kids. In reality, we were anything but. At the camp I attend the summer I turn thirteen, my bunkmates really are spoiled rich kids. One girl insists that she does not have to make her bed because her father is a congressman. Another has a temper tantrum every time fish is served. I am totally shocked by their behavior and tell my parents on Visiting Day that we at Little Red would never behave this way.

Defying the caricature, schools like Little Red, the Francis Parker School, the Park School in Buffalo, the Lincoln School, the Shady Hill School in Cambridge, and the school at Arthurdale rejected the equation learning = work = drudgery. Instead, they wove work, play, and learning together so seamlessly that it was often impossible to tell them apart.

"Children should learn by doing" is a slogan long associated with Dewey and progressive education. When, however, I googled this idea, I found *Wikipedia* saying, "Learning-by-doing is a concept within economic theory. It refers to the capacity of workers to improve their productivity by regularly repeating the same action." This definition is as far from Dewey's idea of learning by doing as one can imagine. When we set type in Miss Eastburn's class, this is not vocational education. When Provenzo and his classmates make and sell cider, they are not in training to be cider makers or shop keepers. When the Lincoln School sixth-grade children make their maps, they are not learning a trade or trying to improve their work skills. We all are simply doing what we must do in order to carry out our projects well, and in the process we are learning our academics.[3]

All schoolchildren learn by doing. The difference is that the things children do in traditional schools—drilling, reciting, filling in blanks on worksheets, reading textbooks, taking notes on what the teacher says, studying for tests—are not authentic real-world activities, each with a history and a cultural niche of its own. They are artificial constructions specifically designed as aids to learning what school is directly teaching.

Building a pueblo, producing a dramatic presentation, putting out a magazine, writing a history book, making cider—the activities progressive schools like Little Red put at the center of the curriculum were not parasitic on school. They were "real life" activities that captured our attention and engaged our interest over extended periods of time. If they were to be done well, we needed all kinds of academic knowledge and skills. And so, while children in traditional schools were learning the three Rs and the various other academic subjects because they were told to—or else because they feared doing badly on tests and in consequence being punished and even kept behind—we were learning them because we needed that knowledge and those skills in order to carry out our projects.

Little Red did not eschew practice and drill. I remember practicing for our weekly spelling tests in the 1os with Sue and recall Miss Kneeland drilling us on the decimal equivalents of fractions in the 13s. The chapter on the 9s in the De Lima book says: "These children love drill. The most popular arithmetic is a speed test, and the arithmetic of the year is largely drill in adding, subtracting, multiplying, and dividing" (1942, 81). But, hear this: "Practical arithmetic is still the core of the year's work. Measuring, weighing, estimating, calculating—are all necessary in planting our bulbs and growing our plants and seeds, and require plenty of practice with quarts, pints, scales, and quantity measures. Arithmetical operations also are necessary in the making of scenery, cutting and fitting patterns for costumes, measuring materials, figuring the amount of cloth necessary for five costumes if one costume needs two yards and a half, figuring the amount of money necessary to buy that many yards if one yard costs twelve cents" (De Lima 1942, 24).

In other words, drill and practice had their place at Little Red, but they did not consume our lives.

Sparing the Rod without Spoiling the Child

One song we never sang at Little Red is the 1907 ditty that begins:

> School days, school days
> Dear old golden rule days
> Readin' and 'ritin' and 'rithmetic
> Taught to the tune of the hickory stick.

The hickory stick is a cousin of the cane Charles Dickens's fictional Mr. Murdstone relentlessly uses on David Copperfield for not knowing his lessons and the one George Orwell's very real teachers wielded when he forgot dates and misread passages. It is a descendent of the ferule that the "school keeper" at Old Sturbridge Village—the living museum in Sturbridge, Massachusetts, that recreates life in rural New England from the 1790s to the 1830s—showed me on my recent visit there with two of my grandsons. And it is closely related to the wooden paddle my husband told me his mechanical drawing teacher in Cincinnati employed—although never on him he assured me—and to the rattan my friend tells me was standard equipment for her teachers in the Boston public school system.

Until the moment of this writing, I was under the impression that such instruments of torture were things of the past. I naively thought that ishment in school had been abolished in the United States. of 2016, it was legal in nineteen states with Mississippi and ιexas accounting for 35 percent of the reported cases. In the school year 2011–2012, 167,000 children received corporal punishment with black students being the recipients far more frequently than whites (Anderson 2015; Ingraham 2016).

In Josephine Tey's *The Daughter of Time*, the detective hero asks the police sergeant who has just arrested a criminal named Chummy what the man is like. "A thorough little bastard," is the reply. "Been treated soft all his life since he started stealing change from his Ma at the age of nine. A good belting at the age of twelve might have saved his life. Now he'll hang before the almond blossoms' out." (1951, 193).

The hickory stick and its relatives are school's version of Sergeant Williams's "spare the rod and spoil the child" philosophy. Or rather, corporal punishment is one form that this time-honored principle takes in school. "Before they resorted to the ferule they used humiliation," the Sturbridge Village school keeper told me. And my friend Lillian says of the parochial school she attended in New Orleans, "They didn't beat us. They humiliated us."

The public humiliation that one of Louisa May Alcott's *Little Women* experiences in school is engraved on my memory. When Amy March breaks a rule by bringing pickled limes into the classroom, her teacher hits her several times on the hand. She bears that pain without flinching, writes Alcott, but when he makes her stand on a platform in front of her classmates for fifteen minutes, she "suffered a pain and shame, she never forgot" (1936, 54). Charlotte Bronte's Jane Eyre underwent a far worse public humiliation at her boarding school. When she accidentally broke her slate, Mr. Brocklehurst made her stand on a stool before everyone for more than thirty minutes and forbade her schoolmates to speak to her for the remainder of the day.

Lillian's humiliation was not quite so severe: she had to wear a large piece of red flannel called "the red tongue" that tied around her head and hung down her neck for most of one day. Googling this badge of dishonor, I learned that the headmaster of an early nineteenth-century English elementary school devised it for children who were too talkative. The New York City public school my friend Florence attended at approximately the same time I was at Little Red employed a different form of punishment. "Obedience was a big thing," Florence told me. "If you were bad you had to stand in the corner. And when the teacher said 'Class, come to attention!' you had to clear your desk off and sit up straight with feet together, arms stretched forward, and hands folded."

So, Heather was right. Mr. Gold could have humiliated her for being unable to tune her violin. For that matter, he could have used the hickory stick. In the world outside school, the "spare the rod and spoil the child" maxim applies to misbehavior. In school the rule has traditionally done double duty: it is invoked when a girl or boy is disobedient, impertinent, inattentive, or unruly *and also* when he or she fails to perform some school assigned task correctly.

Progressive schools like Little Red shunned the spare the rod philosophy altogether. Whether the problem was a fight on the playground or bad spelling, water pistols in class or a mistake in arithmetic, coming late to school or a lack of success in tuning a violin, they tried to navigate a course whose efficacy, indeed even its existence, the spare the rod philosophy denies—a middle way between the Scylla of being harsh and punitive and the Charybdis of coddling.

Our water pistol fight on the roof and Mr. Marvin's talks with Henry and Ann were instances of Little Red's middle way discipline. Banishment by Mr. Marvin to the tiny area next to our classroom—we called it the "chicken coop"—was another. I still remember being dispatched there for talking too much to my neighbor and feeling put upon for being unfairly singled out. My main concern was that I was being made to spend time apart from my friends. Now that I think about it, there was method in Mr. Marvin's madness: between the chicken coop and our classroom was a window through which I could see everyone having a very good time.

Our teachers were not perfect. According to one classmate, "The teachers there were the most rigid in the creative areas. Yeah. I mean, there was, to my mind an emphasis on producing whatever it was they have in mind and very little patience for those of us who just weren't able to do this." I, in turn, have always felt that our art and clay teacher was much too laissez-faire, and one of my classmates concurs. There was "a laissez-faire feeling about art" she tells her interviewer:

In the shop class if you got into trouble and you needed to learn something somebody told you, but in art it didn't seem to me that anybody ever taught you anything. And after a while I got kind of bored. And one of the things I discovered, which of course has nothing to do with art, has everything to do with science was that if you drew a line with paint and you dripped paint on it, it will follow the line and that was really cool. It was cool for a while, but ... it was really boredom. And I'm not sure whether it wouldn't have been better for somebody to, when I wanted it to teach me something.

She adds: "Clay was a little bit like art. I, as somebody who didn't have huge talent, I felt that I was sort of, I could have used more structure."

In retrospect, I can also see that Miss Eastburn let us go too far. Among schoolchildren—whether they are in traditional or progressive schools is immaterial—it is a truth universally acknowledged that some teachers are better at controlling their classrooms than others. I do not recall us trying to push Mr. Marvin or Mr. Stevenson too far or Miss Kneeland any distance at all. Miss Eastburn was another matter. The fourth-grade teacher whom the children in Florence's New York City public school treated badly "was old and fat" and wore "a musty purple dress almost every day" (Freed 2007, 39). Miss Eastburn had no such handicaps and I would have thought her great height was in her favor. Yet, several classmates recall our reducing her to tears.

In the compelling school memoir *Teacher*, Mark Edmundson writes: "It was the natural instinct of the Medford High School student, particularly if male, to push any teacher as far as possible. The English teacher, Miss Cullen, had been brought to tears by our stealing her glasses, our purloining her rank book, our locking her supply closet.... You needed in order to maintain the dignity of yourself and the race of your fellow students, to do what damage you could to the teacher's evolving program but do it without getting identified as a standout miscreant, crucifixion material in the making" (2002, 25–26).

In comparison to Edmundson and his schoolmates we, the Little Red School House class of '43, were rank amateurs at making a teacher's life miserable. Still, we were not nearly so kind to Miss Eastburn as we could and should have been. In the 11s, we talked to our neighbors much too much during class discussions, passed too many notes to our friends, and threw too many spitballs.

The only thing I can say in our defense, and I realize it is no defense at all, is that we were not trying to sabotage her "evolving program" and cannot have done it serious damage. Florence reports that the teacher they persecuted "was a whiz at math, making long division seem a most logical and fascinating exercise" (Freed 2007, 39). While writing this book I have come to appreciate what a whiz Miss Eastburn was. She may not have mastered the art of classroom control. Yet, she is the person who taught us about 1066. It was in her class that we put on our play about the Black Death. Under her guidance we learned how to use the printing press. And she was the one who guided our publication of "The Composing Stick" from the moment we sat down to write our poems and compositions and make our linoleum cuts until the magazine came off the press.

Were We Prepared?

When one of my classmates is asked if she has suggestions on how the interviews could be improved, she replies: "You didn't say to me 'Do you think that Little Red prepared you for your next school?' That, in a sense, did this kind of an education leave you sort of behind the eight ball or able to really function well." Her answer to what in our day would have been "The $64 question" and by now would be the $64,000 or maybe even the $64,000,000 question would have warmed the cockles of Miss Irwin's heart.

The De Lima book says: "If in the primary years we can build up sound and wholesome habits of thinking and of acting, if we can give the child emotional security and when he is ready for them provide him with the few tools which he will need in order to acquire necessary subject matter, education later will have a sound basis on which to build" (1942, 6). Did my classmate think that Little Red had left her behind the eight ball? "Oh, for me, it was fine. I always felt that wherever I went I had been well prepared. That I might have been missing a little piece of information, or a technique, but that generally I knew how to think and how to look at a problem and how to deal with it." This is the same person who tells her interviewer that when her family moved away from New York in the middle of the 12s and she arrived at her new public junior high school, she wrote a book report: "It was ten pages long and didn't have one paragraph because nobody had ever taught me paragraphs. I mean, we were all into such creative writing in school that nobody bothered with things like indentations and breaking off at the end.... When the teacher called me in and said, 'There is no paragraph in ten pages,' I said I didn't know what a paragraph is. She told. After that I used paragraphs. It wasn't too difficult."

I am not so sure that Little Red neglected paragraphs. De Lima says, "Each year paragraphing, question marks, finer and more specific writing forms are emphasized and demanded by the teacher" (1942, 142) and a number of the compositions in *Pen in Hand* contain them. On the other hand, I have no recollection of learning anything about paragraphs until my English A instructor in college told us that a paragraph should be two-thirds of a page long—a rule I followed religiously until a colleague of mine in the English Department at the University of Massachusetts Boston said, "Oh no, it should be half a page."

Perhaps my classmate and I were not paying attention when paragraphs were being discussed. Possibly the instruction was carried out so informally that we were not aware of it. Or maybe our teachers thought she was not yet ready to learn about them at the time she left Little Red. Whatever the reason for her paragraph deficiency, my classmate had some catching up to do in her new junior high, and she did it.

Other members of my class have similar stories to tell about leaving Little Red:

> Well, I came into a very traditional public school [from the 10s at Little Red]. The principal was a retired army officer from South Carolina and the teachers were all appalled that they had a progressive student from New York. The handwriting teacher was appalled that I didn't know how to write cursive, and the math teacher was appalled that I was behind.... The letter from Elisabeth Irwin stated that I had successfully completed fifth grade and was ready to go to sixth grade and there were no grades accompanying which totally shocked him. And he said, perhaps we better put her back. And my mother said, I think it would be a good idea to put her into sixth grade and see what happens, which he did and ... he called her up three weeks later and said, she seems to be quite advanced. We would like to promote her into the next half grade.

> I went to a school [from the 12s at Little Red] where I had Latin, I had algebra, I had severe grammar, and none of which I had any

grounding in whatsoever. It was quite the contrary. And while the initial experience was pretty tough, that I didn't do very well ... the transition [from the 12s] went surprisingly smoothly. And I've always sort of given a lot of credit to Little Red for that.

Well, [in the 13s] I passed the exams to Brooklyn Tech and Bronx Science and Stuyvesant which were, I think at that time there were only four schools in New York that had exams, Music and Art was the other one, so I had to be capable.

I think they [Little Red] gave me a very good grounding in math.... And then by the time I got to high school I was ready for algebra and I was able to do plane geometry on my own and I wanted to do solid geometry and trigonometry I did that ... so yes, I went on to college math.

I was not academically prepared [for high school] ... because I hadn't had algebra, I hadn't had Latin, and I hadn't had French.... But I was able to move ahead and move into them, and without floundering too badly.

Not everyone felt that Little Red had prepared them well enough for their next school. On another of those afternoons my classmates and I spend at Café Vivaldi, one man assures us that he would never send his six-year-old son to a school like Little Red. In his interview he says, "I would never want a child to repeat this kind of education. None of my children have or will." When asked for clarification he explains, "Well, there was a great drawback of this education because there was a lot of things I didn't learn and I had to make up if I wanted to get along and have some kind of schooling."

"In retrospect," another man says in his interview: "I regretted very much that we didn't have any homework.... I had been doing homework in New Jersey, but I lost that skill [at Little Red], and it served me very poorly later on. There was homework at [his high school], but I was not in the habit of it ... and by the time I got to college I got myself into a bit of academic difficulty because I wasn't accustomed to studying outside of the classroom." He also reports:

We had something called Creative Writing. Everybody would have paper and pencil and some period of time, and at the end of the time you turned in what you had written. And the next time around in the class the teacher would read some of the good ones. Well, I usually handed in blank pieces of paper ... nobody seemed to care very much that I was turning in blank pieces of paper. They were *aware* of it obviously. Nobody made a big issue of it. And when I got to college, in freshman English, I wasn't handing in the required writing! I mean, I had gotten into the habit and it led to difficulty.

When I got to college I too blamed Little Red for what I perceived to be enormous deficiencies in my training. At Radcliffe—and this means Harvard since my now defunct alma mater was then its "women's adjunct"—practically everyone except me knows how to study for finals, knows how to write essay exams, and knows what grades mean. I soon discover that grades mean a great deal to them and absolutely nothing to me.

In my sophomore year, a friend and I study together for an upcoming exam in a course called "Democratic Theory and Its Critics." By now I know that the way to do this is to look up previous exams—they are on reserve in the library—and write out answers to the questions on them in advance. It is almost guaranteed that the questions on this year's exam will have been asked in the last two or three or possibly four years. I am sitting cross-legged on the floor in my dormitory room while a graduate of one of the most traditional secondary schools in the country reads my answer to a sample question. "You did not discuss ... ," she says in dismay and tells me everything I did not mention. "Am I supposed to?" I say stupidly. "The question is about Pareto. Why should I mention Freud and Green?" "They're in the course," is her reply. "But first you have to separate out each part of the question. Then you have to answer each part in order. And you have to put in *everything* you know. *Absolutely everything.*"

My Little Red classmate used paragraphs after being told how, and after this informal tutorial I began writing decent exams. Did the ease with which I caught up allay my anger at Little Red? Not at all. The man who said he would not under any circumstances send his children to a school like Little Red reports that in college, "every student took a series of tests that lasted a week when they first got there. And the test consisted of all the finals given in all the courses the previous year and if you got a C in any one of them you didn't have to take the course. There were obviously some kids who matriculated in a week. I had to take every course, including remedial English." The placement tests I took during Radcliffe's orientation week required me to take more French and to me this was proof that my Little Red School House education was sadly lacking.

It is a mystery why, all those years later, the three of us blamed our problems in college on Little Red rather than on our high schools. It is also puzzling why we were as bothered as we were by having had to do some catching up in college. We did catch up. I learned how to study and write exams, and I survived French E. True, I had to take freshman composition but so did 96 or 97 percent of my college class, and few of them had gone to progressive schools. I presume it did not take my classmate too long to learn to study and hand in his homework on time, for he managed to graduate from both college and medical school. As for the man who did not ace his orientation week exams, he ended up with a bachelor's and a master's degree.

Culture Shock and Assimilation

"That was a culture shock, I'll tell you," says a man in my class about his transition from Little Red to one of New York's exam high schools. "It was culture shock! It was remarkably different. I was stunned," says a woman who left Little Red after the 10s for a "quite prestigious school" where "everything was so ordered.... Class lasted from now to now, and lunch hour was here to here, and study hour was here to here, and everything was just—I can't explain it! You couldn't talk up in class, you know. You couldn't do all these things that I was used to doing."

Speaking for myself, I didn't know that what I was experiencing was culture shock. I don't think I had the concept when I arrived at college. Nevertheless, my classmates' comments make me see that this is what I too underwent.

Everyone at Radcliffe but me seems prepared for what I initially perceive as sheer craziness. They take copious notes on utterly boring lectures, memorize the name of Sir Gawain's horse, and display no surprise at being assigned one huge Russian novel per week. I have to figure out how to survive. While I am learning the mores of this foreign culture I am too busy to ask myself if we at Little Red learned anything worthwhile during those years my college classmates spent getting prepared—let alone if all that preparation was necessary. By the time I have learned the ropes, my assimilation into my new culture is so complete that those questions do not cross my mind.

And here is an interesting memory lapse. In the 1970s, I began collecting case studies of whole person transformations brought about by education, and in 2007 I published a book on the subject. I drew my cases from fact and fiction, and one of the first I found was Rita, the hairdresser in Willy Russell's play "Educating Rita" who enrolls in the Open University and is transformed. Did it occur to me when I wrote *Educational Metamorphoses* that just as Rita gradually takes on the attitudes, values, and behavioral patterns of academe, in my first year at Radcliffe I became a convert to traditional education? Absolutely not!

My transformation is not as radical as Rita's. She has to change the way she walks, talks, eats, and dresses in order to fit in and I do not. Yet, not only do I internalize the belief shared by almost everyone around me that Harvard's blood, sweat, and tears approach to learning is the one right way, but I also become convinced that the job of K–12—or at least of grades 1–12—is to prepare children for courses like the one the dean cautioned me against, Harvard's backbreaking History 1. And just as Rita becomes alienated from her husband and her former life, I conclude that despite my having loved Little Red and not withstanding all those happy school days, the education I had there was indeed sub par.

The first glimmer that I have become too critical of progressive education occurs the year I am a teacher in a Massachusetts public school. I have succeeded beyond my wildest dreams. I have gotten my fifth graders so interested in commas—where you put them in and where you don't—that they are practically leaping out of their chairs wanting to be called on. I ought to be ecstatic since commas are not one of my strengths. Instead I am riddled with guilt. To me the miracle I have wrought is a travesty—probably even immoral. There are things in the world to be passionate about—for instance, the prevention of nuclear war and the eradication of racism—and commas are not among them. Besides, shouldn't children learn to write poetry and prose before they worry about where commas go?

Having majored in government at Radcliffe, I consider myself especially qualified to teach social studies. The curriculum for fifth grade consists of a long list of concepts, and so far as I can determine, my job is very simple. I am to teach twenty-five children the definitions of "mountain," "longitude," "the Boston Tea Party," and so on. I know I should be pleased to be passing so much knowledge down to them. Instead, I am horrified at the thought of filling their minds with a long list of unrelated facts that will in all probability have zero meaning for them.

Music is what I know best, and the very nice music supervisor has given me a book of songs for my class to learn. They are surprisingly tuneless but that is the least of my problems. The children are supposed to learn to sight sing, and to that end they and I are to pretend that these are songs without words. We must sing them with solfège syllables—do, re, mi, and so on. I can do this. In the music school of my youth, Mrs. Harris and Miss Goldstein taught us to use numbers of the scale rather than these syllables, but the one system of sight singing easily translates into the other. However, my sight singing courses were in a music school. Although we students were young, we were there to get a specialized education. My fifth graders are not would-be musicians, and I am making them hate music. So, I solemnly promise that if they will do solfège once or twice for each assigned song and impress the supervisor when she next appears, I will let them sing the words. We just won't tell her. They are so happy you would think I had bought each child an ice cream cone. By the time I locate the one decent piece of music in the whole book and enlist the cornet players in the class to help us out, music has become one of this fifth grade's favorite subjects.

Meanwhile, an art specialist arrives weekly to tell my students what they must draw and gives them instructions about how to proceed. The two main rules are: (1) you should always start in the middle of your sheet of paper and then fill up the whole space; (2) you must finish your picture by the end of this period. I am well aware that the one child to disregard them—each week he starts in a corner of his sheet and works outward and he takes an entire week to finish his drawing—is by far the best artist in the group.

I am deeply ambivalent. From having been in Mr. Marvin's class, I know full well that fifth graders should not have to suffer all these indignities. Yet, my Ivy League education has taught me that my early education was not up to snuff. Besides, this is scarcely the moment for me to rekindle my enthusiasm for progressive education. I have been working for a master's degree in education on the theory that it is the way to increase my pitiful salary, and in my very last course I have fallen in love with analytic philosophy. Going on the assumption—where I ever got this idea I do not know—that expertise in this area will give me the tools to improve the town's social studies curriculum, I am leaving school teaching to study philosophy. Where do I plan to do this? At the very institution that drummed into me—not in so many words but by its practices and expectations—how deficient my Little Red education was.

In 1961 I emerge with a Radcliffe/Harvard PhD and whatever thoughts I may once have harbored that progressive education is really not so bad have been effectively squelched. En route I have learned to write a decent essay. The Rousseau to Dewey to Miss Irwin tradition predicts that when you have a "felt need" it is not that difficult to learn something. In college I really and truly felt the need to write decent exams and I learned how. If anything is required to succeed in the field of analytic philosophy, it is essay writing: journal articles are the common currency. And so I take as models two essays my professors have assigned in class and soon figure out what I have to do. I am by now such a fan of traditional education that this vindication of Little Red's philosophy utterly escapes me.

It takes a war to turn me around—or at least to start me on my journey home. In the late 1960s I am on the faculty of the Harvard Graduate School of Education. Students throughout the nation are protesting the Vietnam War and attacking their universities for supporting the military. They want to have a say in college and university governance and they would also like their courses to be more relevant and meaningful. The two senior men in my area—I am terminally junior—are horrified. I am not.

I do not know if these colleagues are reading the current best sellers that say this nation's schools are no better than prisons and that children are being taught to fail. It is beginning to dawn on me that my take on the world of education is different from theirs and from that of almost everyone else in my field. Whatever first premises these philosophers start from—religious doctrine, metaphysical assumption, the definition of man, the needs of society—they end up supporting the selfsame school curriculum that they studied when young! The idea that there could be other approaches to schooling does not seem to occur to them. It does to me.

In 1972 I join the Philosophy Department at the University of Massachusetts Boston. Almost all our students are graduates of Boston area public and parochial high schools and have had firsthand experience of the kind of education the radical school reformers of the day are calling shameful. The men and women in my philosophy of education classes want to be teachers, and they assure me that they are in revolt against the schooling of their youth. When, however, I ask them to contemplate alternative forms of schooling, they are wary. "It's a dog-eat-dog world out there," says one. "You need to be prepared or you won't make it. I hated school. It was a joke. But at least it prepared me." The rest agree.

I say to my students: "I am your professor and I went to one of those 'other' sorts of school. Would I be standing here if my schooling had not prepared me for the real world?" They can scarcely believe that the woman who is going to grade them went to a school without grades, prizes, gold stars, competitions, and rattans. When they ask me if I had trouble adjusting to the dog-eat-dog world, I think for a while. "You learn fast," is what I finally say. Do I realize that I have just defended Little Red against my own criticism of it—the one that caused me to turn my back on progressive education when I did not pass out of French? No, only in writing this book have I come to see where my thinking went wrong.

I blamed Little Red for shortchanging me with respect to my academic education, yet it is fair to say that I was as prepared as the next college freshman to understand the material in our courses. The school had simply not initiated me into the practices Harvard and most other institutions of higher learning employ to teach that material. In other words, except possibly for French, my catching up had nothing to do with the *substance* of my early education. I did not need remedial work in the academic subjects. My deficits were related to higher education's pedagogy and value system—really, its ethos. I had to learn how to take notes in lecture courses, write exams, and compose academic essays. In other words, I needed to learn how to do the activities I had to do in order to get decent grades. And yes, I had to learn to care about grades and to measure people's worth by them.

To this day I believe that my college experience was invaluable and that I could not have done my life's work without it. But being a philosopher of education or a philosopher of anything else is not most people's calling. Suppose it is true—and I am not at all sure it is—that everyone would benefit at some point in their lives from a blood, sweat, and tears approach to learning. Are grades K–8 the appropriate time and place?

Dewey is famous for saying, "Education is not preparation for life; education is life itself."[4] Actually, school is both: it is life here and now *and also* preparation for life after school is done. Little Red believed that initiating us into the culture of mainstream higher education would greatly reduce the quality of our life in school and that we could learn the "tricks of the trade" when we needed them. And Little Red was right.

I wish I had not become so assimilated that I abandoned my belief in progressive education. I regret spending all those years resenting my early training instead of realizing that we were the lucky ones and my college classmates were the people who had been shortchanged. Would that I had understood early on that the main reason they did not resent their elementary and junior high schools for having so often been a joyless, humdrum, humiliating experience simply was that they had no idea it could be otherwise! If only I had known all along what I have learned from telling this story: that Little Red gave us the greatest gift a school can give—a good life filled with the excitement of learning.

Notes

1. Miss Irwin's coauthor was Louis A. Marks.

2. According to Engel et al., "There have been shifts in both public discourse and public policy toward an increased academization of kindergarten with the focus primarily centered on reading instruction" and kindergarten teachers have reported "dramatic increases in time spent on reading between 1998 and 2006. Further, they reported a rise in teachers' expectations with regard to children's school readiness skills across content areas during this period" (2016, 293).

3. The Lincoln School teachers make it clear in De Lima et al. (1942) that their students also had regular periods in their weekly schedule for arithmetic, reading, spelling, and so on.

4. I have not been able to verify that Dewey actually said this. Moreover, it embodies the very kind of "either/or" thinking Dewey ordinarily condemned. But see, for example, Dewey (1961, 239–40).

3   The "We've Been There and Done It" Fantasy

If John Dewey Came Back as a Ghost

My husband loved to tell me how his mother read Dale Carnegie's *How to Win Friends and Influence People* and talked ever after about turning a lemon into a lemonade—transforming a negative situation into a positive one. Progressive education's critics have done the opposite. As skillfully as a magician pulls a rabbit out of a hat, they have turned a lemonade into a lemon.

The basic premise of my story about my classmates' and my school-days emerges from the idea I developed in *Cultural Miseducation* that the large human groupings we call nations have cultural as well as economic wealth. My reason for telling it is that the experiment in which the Little Red of our childhood participated is one of the United States' most valuable cultural assets. As such, it deserves to be passed down from one generation to the next as a treasure trove from which parents and teachers, politicians, and school officials can draw inspiration.

In 1932, the *New York Times* published a series of articles about the parents' decision to establish the Little Red School House as an independent progressive school. A lifetime later someone who had not been on the scene would never know that experiments in education like the one conducted at Little Red had ever taken place.

In 2012, I had the following conversation with my grandson Gabe, then a sixth grader in a Connecticut public school:

JANE: How's school?

GABE: Pretty good.

JANE: "Pretty good" is not as good as "good." Why didn't you say "good"?

GABE: School's irrelevant.

TIM (GABE'S FATHER): You're studying science. That's relevant. What are you learning?

GABE: Density.

JANE: How do they teach it?

GABE: You have a work sheet [he recites a problem off the top of his head that Jane, whose last physics class was in 1946, can barely grasp].

TIM [HOPEFULLY]: And the teacher gives you examples?

GABE: No, you do the problems and you're tested.

TIM: What about social studies? That's always relevant.

GABE: We learned about the Sumerians and cuneiform writing.

TIM: Nothing is more important than literacy and different forms of writing.

JANE: Does your teacher talk about the revolution in writing and literacy that we are now in the middle of?

GABE: No, we read something and then we're tested.

Earlier that day, Tim and I picked up Max, an eighth grader, at his Connecticut public school. Arriving promptly at 2:30 p.m. we waited, as instructed, in a small office where not even the receptionist nodded in our direction. Every so often a large imposing man in a grey business suit ushered a child into or out of an inner chamber. "Who is he?" I later ask my grandson. "The enforcer," is his reply. "Is that what everyone calls him?" I ask. "No," Max says. "It's what I call him." When I report this conversation to my husband he informs me that "enforcer" is a gangster term and reads me *The New Dictionary of American Slang's* definition: "A person, especially a gangster or an athlete, assigned to intimidate or punish opponents" (Chapman 1986).

These are not the only early twenty-first-century schools to embrace the pedagogy that progressive education sought to replace. In 2013, an editor at the *New York Times* wrote: "Let children play games that are not educational in their free time. Personally, I'd rather my children played Cookie Doodle or Cut the Rope on my iPhone while waiting for the subway to school than do multiplication tables to a beep-driven soundtrack.

Then, once they're in the classroom, they can challenge themselves. Deliberate practice of less-than-exhilarating rote work isn't necessarily fun but they need to get used to it—and learn to derive from it meaningful reward" (Paul 2013, SR4). Shortly thereafter, a professor of education commented in the *Times*, "Raising test scores *is still* the mantra of every school reformer" (Reese 2013, SR8, emphasis added). And the following year the *Times* published a letter from a psychologist saying: "Visit any classroom. What you'll find are teachers repeatedly saying 'look up, 'listen' and 'sit still'" (Rao 2014, A20).

My classmates and I were in the 13s when we read the Rosemary and Stephen Vincent Benet poem about Nancy Hanks, Abraham Lincoln's mother, that begins:

> If Nancy Hanks
> Came back as a ghost,
> Seeking news
> Of what she loved most,
> She'd ask first
> "Where's my son?
> What's happened to Abe?
> What's he done?"

In the last verse of the poem Nancy Hanks's ghost asks:

> "You wouldn't know
> About my son?
> Did he grow tall?
> Did he have fun?
> Did he learn to read?
> Did he get to town?
> Do you know his name?
> Did he get on?"

Dewey has often been called the father of progressive education. He, however, insisted that Colonel Francis W. Parker merited that title (Cremin 1961, 21, 129). Dewey published the influential *The School and Society* in 1899 and *The Child and the Curriculum* followed in 1902. By then, Parker had reformed the Quincy, Massachusetts, schools and moved on to being the principal of a teacher training institution in Chicago where he developed his progressive pedagogy further and was able to try it out.

So far as I am concerned the laurels for siring progressive education can go to Parker, Dewey, both of them, or neither. The fact is that well over a century ago an alternative to the traditional academic curriculum and the idea of school as a place of rote learning, testing, and grading was being created in the US. Progressive education was no passing fancy like the Charleston of the 1920s or the Hula-Hoop in the 1950s. According to Cremin, by the end of World War II it was the "conventional wisdom" (1961, 328).

Parker died in 1902, but Dewey lived to see his child "get on" and in good parental fashion to chide it for its excesses (Dewey 1938). If, however, either man came back as a ghost seeking news of the kind of education he loved most, he would be dismayed to learn that mainstream America has all but forgotten the progressive schools of yore.

The two would no doubt be pleased that some schools today—the Little Red School House and Elisabeth Irwin High School among them—proudly call themselves "progressive." But Parker and Dewey would grieve for this country's young were they to discover that a 2013 feature article in what is arguably this nation's leading newspaper takes it for granted that school is a place where you engage in "less-than-exhilarating rote work" and "focus on plain old boring work sheets and exams" (Paul 2013, SR4). They would be scandalized to learn that raising test scores is the mantra of today's school reformers, for that was never their goal. I dread to think how they would feel were they to know that children are still being told to sit still and look at the teacher. Above all, they would mourn for our democracy. How possibly can it survive, they would ask, when schools are judged almost entirely according to how well their students perform on tests of reading, math, and science?

I ask myself the same question. Children are not born believing in democracy and knowing how to make it their way of life. These are acquired characteristics. If twenty-first-century America were a place where children breathed democracy in with the air at home, in their neighborhoods, and at the mall, perhaps schools would not have to make education for democratic living a part of their business. But the United States today is not such a place and I, for one, am deeply concerned that in our all-consuming desire that our children get high test scores, they are not learning "the basics" of democracy.

Conventional Wisdom versus Prevailing Practice

Progressive education has always had its critics. Parker's Quincy, Massachusetts, school system was condemned for neglecting the fundamentals even as evidence accumulated that the children were excelling in reading, writing, spelling, and arithmetic (Cremin 1961, 130). Progressive schools were being called "crime breeders," "time-wasters," and "play houses" at the very time they were reaching their "high-water mark" (Cremin, 324). During World War II, progressive education was increasingly attacked (Zilversmit 1993, 86) and in the 1950s it was blamed "for the nation's disgraceful lag in producing scientists" (Zilversmit, 169). Today the nay saying has changed. Rather than being called an imminent threat to God and country, progressive education is regarded as a failed experiment.

If it were true that we as a nation tried out progressive education and it was a disaster, I would be the first to say that it should be treated as a well-intentioned idea that is best forgotten. But this is pure fantasy. Cremin assured readers of his landmark history that the sources were "legion" for his judgment that progressive education was widely accepted in the United States by the end of World War II (1961, 329). However, he put his faith in professional journals, educational textbooks, school board reports, official publications, and policy announcements, and two well-regarded historians have since shown that these were not reliable informants of actual classroom life.

Using photographs of classrooms, textbooks, recollections of students, teacher reports, the observations of classroom visitors, student writings, research studies, and descriptions of classroom architecture and design, Larry Cuban gathered descriptions of more than 1,200 US classrooms from 1890 to 1990. On the basis of these, he concluded that although incremental changes did occur in the nation's school system, only a minority of teachers actually adopted fundamental alternatives to standard teaching methods and they did so sporadically (1993, 145).

It is said that a picture is worth a thousand words. Arthur Zilversmit's book *Changing Schools*, published in 1993, contains photographs taken just before World War II—in other words, at the "high-watermark" of progressive education—of classrooms that say it all. Sure enough, the desks are arranged in rows and the children are sitting at them with their hands folded and their eyes on the teacher.

So, yes, many private progressive schools were established in the first half of the last century and some public school systems also translated the Parker/Dewey philosophy of education into practice. But the Cuban and Zilversmit research gives the lie to the belief that the United States as a nation has been there and done progressive education.

On the tenth anniversary of the start of the Iraq War, one commentator wrote: "What I remember about that time is the utter impenetrability of the elite pro-war consensus.... It didn't seem to matter what evidence critics of the rush to war presented: Anyone who opposed the war was, by definition, a foolish hippie. Remarkably, that judgment didn't change even after everything the war's critics predicted came true" (Krugman 2013, A17). A similar story can be told about the antiprogressive education consensus. The first edition of Cuban's study of American classrooms was published in 1984, and the second appeared in 1993, the same year as Zilversmit's study. Nonetheless, prominent historians of education have continued to write as if America's conventional wisdom became its prevailing practice.[1]

I ask you: if our nation's schools had all gone progressive after World War II, would I have witnessed what I did in 1952? Like those visitors who used to walk single file into our classrooms at Little Red and observe our every move, I sit with other teaching apprentices against one wall of a Massachusetts elementary school classroom and can scarcely believe my eyes. I take the bolted down desks and glassy eyed children in my stride. But there in the back row is a girl with blood pouring—absolutely pouring—out of her mouth and there in the front of the room stands the teacher, and *he does not see.* Every passing minute I tell myself, "He's not a beginner. He's experienced. He will notice, he will do something about it." But the girl says nothing, the blood keeps gushing, the other children stay eyes front, and the teacher keeps talking, talking, talking until the bell rings.

I ask you: would those best-selling books of the 1960s and 1970s by John Holt, Jonathan Kozol, and others have likened schools to prisons and accused them of teaching children how to fail and boring them to death if the nation's schools had become progressive? No, school's critics would have complained that children were being given too much freedom, not too little. They would have said that school is not supposed to be a place where children have fun.

My experience as a college professor also belies the "we've been there and done it" myth. I joined the University of Massachusetts Boston Philosophy Department in 1972 and for twenty years taught its philosophy of education course every semester to anywhere from fifty to seventy students. If this nation's schools had put progressive education into practice, would I have been the only person in my classrooms who had not gone to a traditional school? Would I have been practically the only one present who was not shocked by what Dewey and Rousseau before him had to say about education? I do not think so.

Edmundson's school memoir depicts his Medford, Massachusetts, high school circa 1969 as an arena of mindless drudgery: "It was a place where you learned to do—or were punished for failing in—a variety of exercises. The content of these exercises mattered not at all. What mattered was form—repetition and form. You filled in the blanks, conjugated, diagrammed, defined, outlined, summarized, recapitulated, positioned, graphed. The subject was of no consequence: English, geometry, biology, history—all were the same" (2002, 5). Would schools have been compared to prisons if Medford High had been the only school of its kind in this nation in the 1960s or if there had been just a smattering of ones like it?

The Linguistic Shift

Some authors know the ins and outs of their plots and subplots before they start writing. Not I. Only after I began work on this chapter did I realize that disregard for the evidence is not the only reason why the fantasy that the United States has been there and done progressive education is widely accepted. Another is that the very meaning of the phrase "progressive education" has changed.

One of the many things I learned from Cremin's history of American education is that the late nineteenth- and early twentieth-century period of social and political reform in the United States known as the Progressive Era spawned a number of educational reform movements. One led to the establishment of the progressive schools of my childhood. Another sought to apply the principles of efficiency and centralization to urban school management.[2] A third wanted to insert vocational training into the public school curriculum. One more tried to ensure that the nation's school system would turn the growing number of new immigrants into loyal citizens.[3]

In years past, the phrase "progressive education" referred primarily to the first reform movement on my list.[4] This and not the other educational reform movements associated with the Progressive Era of American history was the direct descendant of Rousseau and the more immediate offspring of Parker and Dewey. In an admirable attempt at clarity, historian David Tyack called the members of this movement "pedagogical progressives" (1974, 197). Yet when I look back on my schooldays, this label seems too narrow. Little Red's pedagogy did indeed differ from that employed in traditional schools. But so did its approach to curriculum and its conception of what life in school should be like. To conceptualize what was, in effect, an alternative vision of school as a type of pedagogy is to reduce it to just one of its multitudinous aspects.

In this book I have deliberately retained the old unambiguous usage and if I could have my way, everyone else would do the same. But it is too late. "Progressive education" and its close relations "progressive educators" and "educational progressivism" are now being used to cover the whole cluster of educational reforms associated with the Progressive Era. In theory this makes sense: these were all *Progressive* Era reforms and they all had to do with *education* so why not call them all "progressive education"? In fact: calling these very different kinds of reforms by the same name sows confusion and leads the unwary to attribute faults to schools like Little Red that they never had.

When Cremin informed his readers that progressive education was by 1945 the common wisdom, he made it clear that he was referring to the pedagogy Dewey inspired (1961, 328). Others have not been as careful.

A relatively harmless instance of the confusion and misunderstanding that can occur when the various educational reforms are brought under the one umbrella appears in Diane Ravitch's widely acclaimed *Left Back*. Ravitch establishes that she is using "progressive education" as an umbrella term when she says, "Progressive education was clearly a complex series of related movements" (2000, 54). Yet under the broad definition of "progressive education," her assertion that Dewey was its "leading spokesman" is just plain false (57). Dewey may have been the leading spokesman of the progressive school movement but he was not the leading spokesman of the whole kit and caboodle of Progressive Era educational reforms. Indeed, he was highly critical of the vocational education movement. In Dewey's opinion, job training was much too narrow a goal for this nation's schools. So yes, he proposed that occupations or activities—take your pick—be placed at the center of the school curriculum. But he did not—I repeat *not*—want them put there for the purpose of training schoolchildren for jobs.

Dewey realized as few others of his time did that the Industrial Revolution was depriving children of what had been a vital part of their education. Children in an earlier day "were gradually initiated into the mysteries" of the work done at home, he wrote in 1899 (1956, 10). In the process, they were trained in "habits of order and of industry, and in the idea of responsibility, of obligation to do something, to produce something, in the world" (10–11) and they also acquired habits of observation, ingenuity, constructive imagination, and logical thought. Thus, when the Industrial Revolution took furniture making, the production of clothing, and the manufacture of soap, candles, kitchenware, and the like out of the home and placed them in factories, it left a gaping hole in children's education. The problem could be remedied, Dewey said, if schools put meaningful work at the center of the curriculum—not drill and worksheets but real-life occupations. The point would not be job training. Work would be the vehicle for instilling attitudes and values, traits and dispositions that every citizen of this nation should possess and that the Industrial Revolution had put at risk.

At the very time my classmates and I were at Little Red, Professor William Bagley of Columbia University Teachers College was telling the world that progressive education ridiculed the virtues of thoroughness, accuracy, and perseverance, and the ideal of good workmanship (Callahan 1960, 358). Had he observed the sixth graders in Teachers College's own Lincoln School make their maps and murals, he would have known better. Had he seen yours truly and five other children demonstrate to the whole of Little Red how to wrap up a mummy, he could not have said what he did. In regard to one of our plays, a classmate tells his interviewer: "The class wrote the script for the play. The class as a whole produced all the props for the play. And then, when it was produced, it was our doing from ground zero, and when the final product was produced, it was totally—I shouldn't say totally—but it was the class that did it."

Like the Francis W. Parker School's history writing and city building projects, the Park School's cider making project, and the replica the second graders built at Arthurdale, the projects my classmates and I undertook, and the ones the sixth graders at the Lincoln School engaged in served as vehicles for learning the very traits Bagley said progressive education ignored. As for Dewey's desire to train us "in the idea of responsibility, of obligation to do something, to produce something, in the world," whether I was in the 10s, the 11s, the 12s, or the 13s, I firmly believed that I had an obligation to do my part well or else the whole class—and quite possibly the whole school—would be the worse for it.

The "It Was a Disaster" Scenario

Would that using "progressive education" as an umbrella term resulted in nothing more harmful than a misleading statement about John Dewey! There are, however, two parts to the claim that the United States has been there and done progressive education: (1) This nation's school system put progressive education into practice. (2) Progressive education was a disaster. The first part flies in the face of the facts, and the second part rewrites history.

In the "it was a disaster" scenario, progressive education dumbs down America and in the process is undemocratic. The author of the best seller *Cultural Literacy* identified Rousseau and Dewey as the villains of the piece. They opposed "the mere accumulation of information," (Hirsh 1987, xv) and our elementary schools are dominated by their "content-neutral" ideas (19). In the version put forward by Ravitch, the dumbing down occurred because the educational reform movements of the Progressive Era were anti-intellectual and, more particularly, anti-academic-curriculum.[5] She summarizes the disaster in the introduction to *Left Back*. "This book argues that anti-intellectualism was an inescapable consequence of important strains of educational progressivism.... As we shall see, whenever the academic curriculum was diluted or minimized, large numbers of children were pushed through the school system without benefit of a genuine education" (2000, 16).[6]

In the dumbing down of America segment of the disaster scenario, the only genuine education is a traditional academic curriculum—what is often called liberal education. Which strains of progressivism caused its presumed dilution? Vocational education is the obvious suspect. Throughout history the aim of liberal education has been conceptualized as the development of mind, and vocational education has been considered the polar opposite of liberal education. It would seem to follow that vocational education is unintellectual and anti-academic, and from this it is but a small step to the conclusion that insofar as the vocational education movement prevailed, America was dumbed down.[7]

It is not altogether clear that the vocational education movement did prevail in the United States, however.[8] Besides, the progressive schools of the past were not vocational. Thus, even if vocational education was in fact responsible for the presumed dumbing down of America, the schools sired by Parker and Dewey are being wrongly accused.

In the disaster scenario, the villain is not, however, vocational education per se. It is the more general phenomenon of "curricular differentiation." Under the old regime, it is said, our nation's schools delivered the same curriculum to all students, and that curriculum was strictly academic. Under the progressive regime, the academic curriculum became the program of choice for college-bound students and just about everyone else was shunted onto a vocational, industrial, or general track (Ravitch 2000, 15).[9] Because the scenario defines genuine education as academic education, it seems to follow that the introduction of curricular differentiation during the Progressive Era did indeed dumb us down.

Let us all remember that the schools sired by Parker and Dewey did not track children. Besides, high school was where the academic curriculum was mainly "housed." Here is an interesting statistic: at the turn of the twentieth century, less that 5 percent of this nation's adolescents attended high school (Ravitch 2000, 20). Assuming one agrees that only those who study an academic curriculum have had a genuine education—and I do not—it follows that the situation in America was dire long before the Progressive Era's educational reform movements got under way. On my reckoning, the 5 percent high school enrollment number in 1900 means that 95 percent of Americans were already being denied an academic education.

With such a high proportion of our population already lacking a "genuine" education—in other words, with America already being in what is claimed to be a dumbed down condition—how possibly could progressive education dumb us down? To rephrase the question: Given the 5 percent 1900 enrollment figure, is it not unfair to hold one or more of the

Progressive Era's educational reform movements responsible for what was actually a pre-existing condition?

The "it was a disaster" scenario employs a double standard. It blames progressive education for not giving every child an academic education and lets everyone else off the hook: even though the situation predated the Progressive Era, and despite the fact that curricular differentiation did not reduce the percentage of adolescents in the total population who were receiving an academic education. In 1928, approximately one-third of high school students were taking nonacademic courses. At that point, however, high school enrollment had risen to just under 50 percent of the fourteen- to seventeen-year-old population and over two-thirds of the ones in high school were still taking academic courses. In 1961, close to 90 percent of adolescents were enrolled in high school, and well over 50 percent remained in academic courses. Thus, although it is true that as the twentieth century rolled on the percentage of public high school students following an academic curriculum decreased, it is also the case that *a larger percentage of Americans than ever before were receiving an academic education.*

The disaster scenario indicts progressive education for being "profoundly undemocratic" as well as anti-intellectual and anti-academic (Ravitch 2000, 15; cf. Hirsch) on the grounds that those who ended up on the new nonacademic tracks were mainly children of the poor, immigrants, and racial minorities. I agree that the tracking of poor people, immigrants, and racial minorities into nonacademic school programs is undemocratic. I also believe that if blame is to be attributed, it should be done fairly. Who attended high school circa 1900? Children whose families had enough resources so that their offspring did not have to go to work on the farm, in factories, or in other people's homes. Who did not attend high school? Children whose families could not afford this luxury. This means that de facto tracking similar to the de jure kind that is being blamed on progressive educators predated the Progressive Era.

Ravitch writes in *Left Back*: "Progressive educators wanted socially efficient schools that would serve society by training students for jobs" (2000, 52). And a few pages later: "Progressive education reformers wanted the public schools to make a significant contribution to the emerging industrial order. They pressed the schools to adjust to the rapidly changing society and to cast aside outmoded assumptions, one of which was the idea that the academic curriculum was appropriate for all children. Progressive educators argued that the bookish curriculum blocked social progress and that it was unfitted to the hordes of immigrant children crowding into the urban schools. These children, the reformers said, needed training for jobs in the industrial economy, not algebra and literature" (54–55).

I do not doubt that some—perhaps even many—educational reformers of the Progressive Era held these views. But the very idea that the nation's schools were filled with "hordes of immigrant children" who needed job training rather than math and literature contradicts everything Little Red represented. I cannot speak for Parker and Dewey, let alone for the founders of all the progressive schools they sired. This elitist and fundamentally undemocratic point of view would have seemed grotesque and have been abhorrent, however, to Miss Irwin and our teachers.

The reddish doors at 196 Bleecker Street were open to all. "Our children are drawn from all walks of life and include descendants of those who came over in the Mayflower and refugee children who have just arrived in this country.... We accept our applicants as they come, without tests and often without an interview, just as public schools do" says De Lima (1942, 7). After describing a visit to the Harlem home of one of his best friends in our class, a white classmate who described himself as a United Methodist says: "We had a number of Jewish children in the class and we also had a young man from Palestine and he had stories of being around the fighting that was going on at that time."

Diversity was built into our daily lives and the acceptance of difference was consciously incorporated into the school curriculum. Few traditional schools of the day could have said as much:

> Well, I think one of the most important things in that era was that we had such a diversified student body, because that was a real contrast to [her high school], where it was all girls, and you know, very few Jews, very few blacks, very few anybody who was the least bit different. Whereas at Little Red—and I've really always been so grateful for that, because I don't—I know that I don't have any feelings about people in relation to the color, their religion, or anything else.

> When I went to [a New England boarding school] ... there was a public speaking prize, the Cup for Public Speaking. And I made a speech [about relegating] the Negro to the back end of the bus. And

I won the prize. And I think this was certainly completely rooted in my experience at Little Red School House.

The De Lima book explains that the study of the ancient Hebrews in the 10s "afforded the children an opportunity to appreciate the problems and contributions of the Jewish people" (1942, 83). Another reason for the unit was that it gave children: "a chance to observe problems more or less common to any minority group. Accepting others who are different from ourselves has been a chief problem of mankind since the beginning of history. It is equally a problem with ten-year-old children. A child in the group who is different from the others is sometimes rejected or persecuted. Such intolerance must, of course, be overcome and one way to do this is to let children see the tragedies which intolerance has caused among peoples in history" (84).

The book also points out that from the study of American Indians, children in the 8s get a sense of "the difference in people and races" and in the chapter on the 13s it says: "we try to be understanding of others. Study of the Negro and the immigrant is included in the curriculum of the thirteens with a special purpose in mind. We wish to go beyond tolerance of another race; we want to learn to understand and appreciate the contribution which this race is making to our American life" (113).[10]

In the chapter entitled "Our Classrooms Have No Walls," Mr. Studer, then teacher of the 13s, wrote about the trips his class took: "It would take a great deal of space to list the different types of people met on these trips. The children talked to rich farmers and poor; to backwoodsmen, technicians, factory workers, hermits, and sandhogs.... A feeling of kinship with people totally different began to develop" (159). In addition, when our behavior fell short of the ideal of equality to which Little Red subscribed, our teachers were quick to step in.

"We want to rid ourselves of the tawdry stereotype to be found in the ordinary work of fiction, movie or radio script, where the Negro is portrayed as a clown, a lackadaisical, shiftless good-for-nothing, or the abjectly devoted menial," it says in De Lima's chapter on the 13s (1942, 113) and when we were in the 13s we found out that our teachers meant it. We all thought one African American boy in our class was extremely funny. He made us laugh by doing things like "accidentally" on purpose falling backward in his chair. One day he did this in Miss Kneeland's class and we got hysterical. What happened next was not so funny, however.

Whether it was the same day or the next I cannot say for sure, but when our classmate was for some reason out of the room and we were sitting in a circle, Miss Kneeland gave us *hell*. I have never forgotten how angry she was at us and have seldom felt so ashamed of myself. I was totally shocked and I think everyone else was too. Basically, she told us that he was acting out a racial stereotype and that we were feeding into this: our laughing was egging him on to do it more. If we were to be the mature citizens of a democracy that we claimed we were, we needed to take him more seriously so that he would take himself more seriously. We must never, ever do that again. "Do you understand what I am saying? Never, ever!"

Rewriting the Past

In November, 2000, Robert Butche, who attended Ohio State's University School, a once famous progressive school, and in 2000 published a book on the subject wrote: "Her [Ravitch's] view of progressivism, its methodologies, practices and philosophies is so distorted as to be unrecognizable to those of us who lived through its heyday here at the Ohio State University."[11] Butche was so offended by what he took to be an attack on the progressive education he knew firsthand that he strongly implied that *Left Back*'s negative account was politically motivated—this, although he apparently shared what he called Ravitch's "conservative political leanings."[12]

I have never shared the quite common assumption that a political conservative will of course be opposed to progressive education. Do not political conservatives want their children to have a good life in school? Do they not want their children to think for themselves?

> One thing [Little Red] taught me was the important thing was not memorizing facts and figures but knowing where to find things if you needed them and learning how to find things for yourself, figure things out, get the resources and the references.

> Their attitude was of developing our minds or our imaginations, and not of pushing in the facts. Well, learning.... I don't tend to jump to conclusions. I don't tend to oversimplify things. I think it's important to look at all sides of an argument. I think it's important to be open to others and their views, their particular backgrounds or that they come from, frame of reference that they come from.

> Beginning to learn to think for yourself I would think is the most positive thing I gained from [Little Red].

> It [Little Red] did give me the ability to think things through, and if I didn't know the answer, well then I could do some research and find out what it is all about, and how to do it, and that sort of thing.

Be this as it may, the linguistic shift has raised the ante. Call the various kinds of Progressive Era educational reforms by the same name and the sins of one type of reform will all too likely be attributed to the others. The mistake is known as "the fallacy of guilt by association," and guilt by association is what has happened.

Butche and I know better than to accept bizarrely distorted portraits of the Parker and Dewey form of progressive education, for we were there. But an enthusiastic Amazon.com citizen reviewer of *Left Back* who was not there had this to say: "However well-meaning, the advocates of progressive education may have been, they have caused terrible harm by holding an array of destructive views, from poisonous social determinism at one end (black students are probably going to grow up to work in menial jobs anyway, so there's no point in teaching them abstract academic subjects they will never need) to loony naturism at the other, under which children should never be taught about anything that they don't ask to be taught about" (O'Hara 2001).

As it happens, there were at least as many different kinds of progressive schools in New York City alone when I attended Little Red as there were different Progressive Era educational reform movements. Whether any of them believed in a "poisonous social determinism" that denied black students access to an academic curriculum I do not know. I am not even sure if any of them gave children the kind of freedom to choose what they would be taught that Summerhill in England did.[13]

To assert that the progressive schools of yore were inescapably anti-intellectual and undemocratic is a false generalization of the first order. Little Red, for one, did not fit into either category. Furthermore, the disaster scenario gives the false impression of where educators in the pre-Progressive Era stood on these issues and where educators in the Progressive Era who opposed school reform stood. Ravitch writes, "Nineteenth-century educators believed that the best way to improve society was to offer a sound education to as many children as possible." She adds, "Progressive educators of the early twentieth century rejected this view as hopelessly conservative, even reactionary" (2000, 76).

No. In the early twentieth century, the members of the progressive movement were the ones who wanted to give as many children as possible a sound education. Jacob Riis, Lincoln Steffens, Ida Tarbell, Louis Brandeis, Jane Addams, Alice Hamilton, Robert M. La Follette, and Theodore Roosevelt—they were the ones who sought to extend democracy to men, women, and children living in poverty, whether native-born or immigrants. What progressive educators like Parker and Dewey rejected was the nineteenth century's definition of a sound education: namely, the standard academic curriculum and its accompanying pedagogy of drill, tests, memorization, gold stars, and the rest.

The suggestion that educators who remained outside the progressive movement were more democratically inclined and egalitarian than those inside is a bizarre reversal of history, and the airbrushed portraits of the traditional academic curriculum that have recently been painted represent a denial of the past. "As used in this book," writes Ravitch, "the term 'academic curriculum' does not refer to the formalistic methods, rote recitations, and student passivity about which all reasonable educators and parents have justly complained" (2000, 150). The truth is that most advocates of the traditional academic curriculum did not complain. Mindless memorization, rote recitations, harsh disciplinary measures, and threats of failing grades for centuries constituted the pedagogy of choice for huge numbers of teachers of the academic curriculum. As for those who did complain, the loudest was Rousseau—the man who is portrayed in the disaster scenario as a misguided romantic. Parker and Dewey were two more highly vocal complainers, and the schools they sired are the very ones the scenario condemns.

In another revision of the past, the scriptwriters give the impression—or rather, the misimpression—that the progressive schools of the first half of the twentieth century were all established by and for the upper classes. In fact, the progressive school at Arthurdale served West Virginia's impoverished coal mining families. When William Wirt introduced progressive education into the public school system of Gary, Indiana, Gary was a heterogeneous working-class city with a large immigrant population (Zilversmit 1993, 57). And Little Red did not fit the description either.

Bob Lilien began his essay on Little Red by assuring his new friends at Stuyvesant that "it is not a rich man's school; it is much to the contrary" (De Lima 1942, 217). Looking back at the founding of Little Red on the fortieth anniversary of its Bleecker Street opening, Mrs. Hawkins—our teacher in the 6s who was there at the start—wrote:

> From the very beginning of our existence as an independent school in September 1932, we believed in and followed a policy of equal opportunity—between the sexes, among the races. No child was to be discriminated against. Our first tuition was $125—for those who could pay. And we left no children behind in P.S. 41 because their parents couldn't afford to pay the fee. Everybody was personally involved in creating the school. All talents and abilities among the parents were offered and gladly received. The first year, at least two dozen gallon-sized paint buckets resided in my room. We worked around them. Parents came at night and on weekends and painted the walls throughout the school. Our cubbies were orange crates. We may not have worried about environmental pollution in those days but we surely had a passion for recycling, and for making something out of nothing.

According to one of my classmates, "We were very poor. I lived in hand me downs from older cousins and I don't imagine any of the kids, or few of the kids from the class were well to do, but I don't think any of them or many of them were really as poor as we were." Said another: "Many of us were what you might call latchkey children. Our parents both worked. Or if you just had one parent they ... you know." A third reported:

> I was just in awe and all these kids [in the school she attended when she left Little Red] were rich. I wasn't rich. They had all gorgeous clothes and I had the same stuff I wore every day ... I think when the kids that were there discovered that my parents were divorced, which was a stigma at that time, and that I didn't have any money, and that I lived in Greenwich Village, I mean as they learned more about me, they were quite snobbish about it. And I didn't have the money that they had. They would buy savings bonds every week and my mother would give us money for a ten-cent savings war stamp,

you know it was during the war, and she had trouble even scraping up the class dues. You know, she had *trouble.*

And one more said: "I remember one boy who had very little money at all. I don't really remember what his father did. Money did not seem to be a criterion for people to attend the school so that we had a wide range of contacts with people of various life experiences."

We, the children, came from a broad economic spectrum and there was nothing elite about the school's location. "Our school is located in a neighborhood which, however picturesque it may be, is a constant reminder of the gross inequalities of our social order," wrote De Lima (1942, 23). The Greenwich Village of our day housed poets and novelists, actors and playwrights, artists and photographers, political activists and social reformers—many of them struggling to make ends meet— and also a large working-class Italian immigrant community. When we walked from our homes and our subway stops to those welcoming school doors, we passed butchers, bakers, barbershops, and pushcarts— not expensive clothing stores. When we marched in a scraggly line to the city playground on Sixth Avenue or hiked further downtown to the lunchroom on Charlton Street, there were no fancy boutiques and world-class museums.

"What exactly did we see on our way to the playground?" I ask when Henry, his wife, and I visit Olga. Olga thinks the playground was right next to the school. I have a vague recollection of some brown building or other. Henry says there was a tenement between the school and the playground. Months later I query Kay Kay and she tells me we used to walk past three tenements.

Henry reminds us that the playground was paved with coal cinders that hurt when they got in your knees, and that inspires me to show off the faded scar on my wrist. "I tried to climb over the chain link fence and got stuck on the top," I boast. Olga is duly impressed and of the opinion that she would not have dared do that. In my memory, she is one of the ones who went over without mishap. In fact, in my memory everyone but me climbed over without mishap.

I did not live in Greenwich Village—something I deeply regretted as a child—but after Mr. Marvin took our class on a walk down MacDougal

Street, I considered Little Red's neighborhood my own. After one such walk, Olga wrote:

A MacDougal Lady

Nose pushed in
Upon the face:
Permanent wave
Done up in lace:

Double chin,
Big wide feet:
Awfully sloppy
And feels the heat.

Dumps the garbage
On the street:
Slops up the stairs
And sits down to eat.

Oily permanent
On top of the head,
Tied with a net
When she goes to bed.

Pimples all over
From ear to ear:
Wears a long coat
And drinks a lot of beer.

But the nose pushed in
Upon the face,
Pimples all over
And the net of lace

Makes her look like an owl
But she is not wise;
And she's got a parrot
And sometimes cries:

"Mama's going to town;
Mama's going to town;

> Mama's going to town;
> In a long black gown;
> In a long black gown;
> In a long black gown. (De Lima 1942, 334–335)

President John F. Kennedy made headlines while campaigning for office when he said that in West Virginia he was seeing poverty for the first time in his life. I suppose I should have admired him for being shocked at the sight. Instead, I was dismayed that it had taken so long for him to see poverty firsthand and kept thinking that if he had gone to Little Red, he would have made its acquaintance much sooner.

Bob Lilien told his public high school classmates about a trip his class went on at Little Red: "In small groups we took overnight automobile trips and visited 'forgotten towns' of New Jersey. We visited child labor conditions in the bogs and got firsthand information from the children themselves" (De Lima 1942, 218). Fifty years later, one classmate of mine recalls how much he regretted that we had not gone on that same trip: "The class ahead of us went to the cranberry bogs in New Jersey. This was during the Depression and they came back with stories about the unemployed; people were living in very poor circumstances and so on. And we did not get to go there the next year and I felt very much deprived, and it obviously still sticks with me."

Fact or Fiction?

My dictionary defines the word "fantasy" as follows: (1) imagination, especially when unrestrained, (2) the forming of grotesque mental images, and (3) a daydream. In its disregard of the facts, the claim that this nation's schools put progressive education into practice fits the first meaning. And the second claim, that it was a disaster, falls under both the first and the second meaning.

I said earlier that if Parker and Dewey came back as ghosts seeking news of what they loved most, they would be dismayed. Actually, they would be aghast. Anti-intellectual, undemocratic, very likely racist, and most certainly elitist, this portrait of the progressive education they sired makes a mockery of everything they stood for. Indeed, the omissions and misinformation so distort our cultural memory that in the course of writing this book I have had to ask myself: What is it about progressive education that makes its critics willing to play havoc with the truth?

This is not the first time that progressive education's critics have portrayed it as the enemy of democracy. In the McCarthy era, critics of progressive education were quick to employ what was then the very real scare tactic of calling it communistic and that practice has persisted into this century. I have in my hand a two-paragraph abstract of an article in a 2005 issue of the magazine *Commentary*. It says that the Little Red School House from its founding "was dedicated to left-wing politics and culture," and that students there "were being inducted into the ideas and prescriptions of the Soviet-organized Popular Front of the mid-1930's one of whose most memorable slogans was 'Communism is twentieth century Americanism'" (Rosenthal 2005). According to the author of a 1998 book called *Raising Reds*, in the 1930s "Communists and their allies began to participate in [progressive schools] as parents, teachers, and administrators" (Mischler 1999, 101).

All I can do is shake my head in amazement. Miss Irwin did not set up her experiment in the New York City school system in order to create young communists; she simply wanted to fit the school to the child. The parents who launched Little Red as an independent school did not meet in the ice cream parlor on Sixth Avenue in order to promote a political ideology; they just wanted their children to continue to be happy while they learn.

Ragoné and I did not think to ask in the interviews if the parents of anyone in the Little Red School House class of '43 were communists. Given that the majority of Communist Party members lived in New York City and that the Bleecker Street school doors opened during the Great Depression, it is a good bet that some children in the school were "red diaper babies." But I estimate that the great majority of parents were, like my own parents, like the great majority of New Yorkers, and like the majority of people in the whole United States—just plain Franklin Delano Roosevelt Democrats. A classmate of mine confides, "I think I grew up with the idea that I was going to be able to vote for Roosevelt for the rest of my life." I know I did.

Not long ago I read a collection of forty-six brief memoirs by former "red diaper babies" and was struck by how many of the authors—more than 90 percent—had *not* gone to progressive schools.[14] I should not have been surprised. The USSR denounced progressive education in the 1930s and one can see why. Rousseau wanted his imaginary boy Emile to think for himself. Dewey wanted children to be able to solve the kinds of problems one faces in everyday life as well as the kind that the citizens of a democracy are called on to solve, and so did Miss Irwin. That is why from day one at Little Red, we children were learning to figure things out for ourselves, examine our own conclusions critically, question received wisdom no matter the source, and act on our beliefs.

A classmate recalls: "They would present a problem and, you know, 'How are we going to do this?' They didn't say how to do it. We had to figure it out, you know get together. 'Let's see how we are going to do this' and we would solve it. And, in that way I think—I don't know, it's hard to explain, but I think you're more alert to the world." Explaining the difference between her high school and Little Red, another says: "You know, we studied opera and we would go to an opera. And it was just such a different thing than singing at Little Red ... It was all sort of do it yourself at Little Red And after that, it became much more—I don't want to say voyeur, but ... spectator. Yeah, spectator, exactly. It's rather than participating."

The great irony of the once fashionable claim that progressive education is communistic is that the school system of the country that symbolized communism when I was young was as traditional as can be. Quite simply, the USSR could not tolerate the thought of a population that engaged in this kind of critical thinking. Teachers in the Soviet Union were expected to transmit standardized content to their students, the students had to memorize said content, classrooms were regimented, and schoolwork was graded. And it worked. It turned out millions of communists.

Those today who tell us that we've been there and done progressive education and it was a disaster are as different from the Soviet educators of the 1930s as can be. Yet their flagrant misrepresentation of the history of American schooling makes me wonder if they too fear the kind of schooling that teaches children to think and act for themselves.

Notes

1. Patricia Graham's *Schooling in America* (2005) repeats Cremin's finding (1961, 66) that "by the end of World War II progressivism was the reigning ideology." Making no reference to the Cuban and Zilversmit studies, her narrative nonetheless conveys the distinct impression that across the country the Parker/Dewey philosophy of education became America's reality. Diane Ravitch mentions the Cuban and Zilversmit research in *Left Back*

but her history of twentieth century school reform is also written as if their findings do not bear on the subject.

2. See Fallace and Fantozzi (2013) for interesting discussions of the social efficiency strand of the Progressive Era's educational reforms.

3. See Shaker (2004) for an extended discussion of Ravitch's conflation of the different kinds of educational reform movements within the Progressive Movement.

4. Zilversmit says: "In arriving at a definition [of progressive education], it is important to recognize that progressive education was only one of several contemporary educational reform movements" (1993, 2).

5. Mirrel (2006) recounts the dumbing down of America without implicating progressive education.

6. In *Reign of Error* Ravitch (2013) twice quotes Dewey with approval. Yet there and elsewhere she supports the very academic curriculum and sequential learning that Dewey spent his life opposing. Wrote Dewey in *Schools of Tomorrow*: "The academic education turns out future citizens with no sympathy for work done with the hands, and with absolutely no training for understanding the most serious of present day social and political difficulties." (1915, 315).

7. See Schultz (2001) for a powerful defense of vocational education.

8. According to Mirrel (2006), by 1920 most big-city high schools had replaced the earlier single-track academic curriculum with a college prep track, a commercial track, a vocational track, and a general track. Yet in 1928 about 67 percent of high school classes remained in the traditional academic areas, in 1934 that number was just over 62 percent, and in 1961 it was 57 percent.

9. For example, Ravitch (2000) writes, "Progressive educators wanted socially efficient schools that would serve society by training students for jobs" (52). And a few pages later: "Progressive education reformers wanted the public schools to make a significant contribution to the emerging industrial order. They pressed the schools to adjust to the rapidly changing society and to cast aside outmoded assumptions, one of which was the idea that the academic curriculum was appropriate for all children" (54–55). Summing up the situation, she says that the progressive education movement "encompassed four significant ideas. Taken together, these ideas undermined the premise that all children should study a solid academic curriculum. Indeed, they raised doubts about the value of a solid academic education for *anyone*" (60, emphasis in original).

10. In my childhood, "Negro" was considered to be a nonracist term.

11. Butche was Historian of Ohio State's College of Education and the author of: *Image of Excellence* (Butche 2000).

12. In the acknowledgments section of *Left Back*, Ravitch reports that her writing of the book was "generously supported" by the John M. Olin Foundation (2000, 534). Jane Mayer *In Dark Money* lists Olin as a member of "a small, rarefied group of hugely wealthy, arch conservative families that for decades poured money, often with little public disclosure, into influencing how Americans thought and voted" (2016, 4).

13. Saying that "progressive educational practice" is based on Rousseau's Noble Savage,— something Dewey would almost surely deny, Pinker (2002, 222) in effect reduces it to the kind of education practiced at A. S. Neill's Summerhill.

14. They attended their local traditionally oriented public schools.

4 Close Encounters of an Educational Kind

Knowledge by Acquaintance

"How come you people remember so much?" asks my husband, who has envied my Little Red classmates and me ever since he accompanied me to that first reunion at Henry's house. "I can't believe you remember all that," Sandy's wife exclaims at one of our Boston area reunions. "I went to P.S. 9 [in New York City] and I don't remember anything."

The great sociologist Karl Mannheim once wrote: "It makes a great difference whether I acquire memories for myself in the process of personal development, or whether I simply take them over from someone else. I only really possess those 'memories' which I have created directly for myself, only that 'knowledge, I have personally gained in real situations. This is the only sort of knowledge that really 'sticks' and it alone has binding power" (1952, 128). I think our memories of Little Red are so strong because we did not acquire our knowledge from someone else. We gained it personally "in real situations."

Philosophers across the ages have asked, "What is truth?," "What is justice?," "What is art?," "What is law?" In my most recent book, *Education Reconfigured*, I asked, "What is education?" My answer was that at rock bottom, education is a matter of the encounters an individual has with culture or, to be more specific, with items of a culture's "stock"—and by *culture* I had in mind not just "high" culture but culture in the broad sense of the term. Strip away the time, the place, the backgrounds of the participants, the pedagogy, the visual aids—in other words, the inessentials—from any educational event. What is left is an encounter between an individual and some portion of cultural stock in which the two become yoked together and both parties—the individual and the culture—change. The change in the individual is what we call "learning," and the change in the culture is what we call "cultural transmission."

Schooling is no exception to this rule. Spelling, grammar, long division, the Bill of Rights, the Norman Conquest, the Golden Rule—every bit of subject matter in a school curriculum, or any other curriculum, is an item of culture and the learning that occurs is a function of the encounters that the children have with various items of cultural stock.[1] When you think about school and ask yourself what is happening to the culture rather than the children, you will perceive items of cultural stock being passed along to the next generation—in other words, cultural transmission.

Mannheim is right. The reason my classmates and I remember our schooldays so clearly—or at least one reason we do—is that so many of our encounters with our school subject matter involved what philosophers call "knowledge by acquaintance." The chapter on the 12s in the De Lima book is entitled "The Twelves Go American," and it speaks of the class "*living again* the life of those early Americans" (1942, 102, emphasis added). That is no exaggeration. When in the 10s I wrapped up our mummy on stage, I truly felt as if I was living again the life of an ancient Egyptian, and when in the 11s my classmates and I reenacted the Black Death and learned to set type, we seemed to ourselves to be right down there on the ground in the Middle Ages. Needless to say, we did not have actual real-life encounters with the ancient Hebrews and Egyptians or the people of the Middle Ages. From the standpoint of long-term memory, however, our teachers gave us the next best thing: they created—and helped us create—what amounted to virtual realities for us to enter.

Computer-based virtual realities require the suspension of disbelief and so of course did our "virtual encounters" with other times, places, and cultures. We knew that we were not really making bricks without straw when in the 10s we sang "Down in the brickyards working all the day," even though we felt as if we were. When my classmates walked down what were once Indian trails with maps in hand, they knew they were really schoolchildren in Greenwich Village. In the 11s, we knew that we were not really dying from the plague. And when in the 12s, I said half the line "It's Mistress Winthrop, the Governor's Wife," I knew I was not really a member of the Massachusetts Bay Colony. Yet, compared to the encounters schoolchildren typically have with their prescribed subject matter, ours were close enough to seem firsthand.

Rousseau said in *Emile*, "I hate books." He did not mean it. After all, he read them, he wrote them, and he referred to them in his writings. But he thought that books are bad for young children because "they only teach one to talk about what one does not know" (1979, 184). You might protest: this is exactly what makes books so good for children. However, Rousseau believed that children should have direct firsthand experience of the world before learning about it from others.

Our teachers agreed. They did not hate books. They loved them, and because they wanted us to love them, they took us on trips to the public library, had us borrow books from the school library, and read aloud to us. Nowhere in the De Lima volume is Rousseau's name mentioned. Yet like Tolstoy, Dewey, and Charles, my father's tutor: Mrs. Hawkins, Miss Stall, Mr. Marvin, Miss Kneeland, and the others were his descendants.

After explaining that the school began formal reading instruction in the 7s rather than the 5s or 6s, the De Lima book says: "To put the main emphasis of the school day upon the acquiring of symbolic language and numerical abstractions when there is so much that a child can get directly from his immediate surroundings is surely a stupid proceeding" (1942, 20). Little Red arranged for us to have knowledge by acquaintance of the world around us, and knowledge *by virtual acquaintance* of those parts of the present world we could not actually visit and also of the world of the past.

Our firsthand acquaintance of the world started in the 5s and 6s with trips around the city and did not stop when formal instruction in the 3Rs began. In the chapter on the 10s in the De Lima book there is an account of my class's creative writing period after we take a trip to Manhattan's Lower East Side. We have just seen the hectic activity of the open-air markets for ourselves. Then, back in school, we children write our poems and compositions.

Our knowledge by acquaintance extended to the natural world. In the chapter on the 9s in the De Lima book it says:

> We go to Central Park to see the glacial rocks and to Inwood Park after a heavy rain to see how water and wind are changing the land now. We have a large canvas which we spread on the floor to hold quantities of damp sand. We talk about the kind of land in Norway and Sweden and build it up ... We go further and discuss Iceland, Greenland, the British Isles, the northern part of Europe, and the northern part of North America. This is done over weeks at intervals; the various places are named, the islands, seas, bays, fjords. (1942, 76)

And two of my classmates report:

> Well, we had lots of sort of hands on experimental work in science and so on, and would sort of grow little seeds, or I remember at one point the experiment was, in those days milk came in glass bottles and the glass bottles had narrow necks and they had us, the winters were cold, so they had us fill some milk bottles with water right up to the top and put them out on the window sill in the cold winter, and we would, you could observe how when the water froze the force of the ice freezing was enough, and expanding, was enough to break the bottles. And they had a lot of ingenious little experiments like that that demonstrated to the children the principles of physics or chemistry or whatever, and those lessons that were remembered.

> We continued with science [at June Camp], by going on science walks, hikes, and collecting scientific objects and articles for our science lab, if you will (it wasn't a lab, but, I mean, it was a place where we collected things). So scientific information. We also collected items that were native to that area, along with the kinds of rocks, plants, (not trees, but bushes we could grow), and that was studying nature. And then, of course by studying nature, we would go through the woods and observe all the things that grow in the woods that you didn't see in the city.

Philosophers contrast knowledge by acquaintance with the kind of knowledge you have when you know that something is the case—for instance that 2 + 2 = 4 or the date of the Battle of Hastings. They also distinguish it from "know how"—the kind of knowledge you have when you can do something such as read, ride a bicycle, play the violin, or add and subtract.

It is often assumed that knowledge by acquaintance is an inferior type of knowledge and that one of the main functions of a good education is to go beyond it. We humans would indeed be in a sorry state if all each one of us had to go on was our own firsthand knowledge. Nonetheless, the fact drilled into most schoolchildren of our generation that Dutch settlers bought Manhattan Island from the Indians for $24 had special meaning for us at Little Red. After all, we had walked the Indian trails. The principle of religious freedom was for us a living legacy because we felt as if we had been standing next to Anne Hutchinson when she was under siege in the Massachusetts Bay Colony. Theodore Roosevelt's biographer reports that he:

considered his experience with "fellow ranchmen on what was then the frontier" to be "the most educational asset" of his entire life, instrumental to his success in becoming president. "It is a mighty good thing to know men, not from looking at them, but from having been one of them," Roosevelt explained. "When you have worked with them, when you have lived with them, you do not have to wonder how they feel, because you feel it yourself." (Goodwin 2013, 125–126)

And the author of the best-seller *Seabiscuit* read vintage newspapers in order "to start to feel like I was living in the '30s" (Hylton 2014, 42).

Nobel Prize winner Barbara McClintock said of her work on corn: "No two plants are exactly alike. They're all different, and you have to know that difference. I start with the seedling, and I don't want to leave it. I don't feel I really know the story if I don't watch the plant all the way along. So I know every plant in the field. I know them intimately, and I find it a great pleasure to know them" (Keller 1985, 164). And the eminent biologist E. O. Wilson told an interviewer: "If you want to explain ants, then you have got to know ants" (Lehrer 2012, 40).

As it happens, in the 10s Jay wrote about a close educational encounter he had with ants:

Ant Hills

One day in a lot near my house, I found twenty or thirty ant hills. To a person who doesn't like ants and walks along the street making a point of stepping on them, an ant hill is a pile of dirt with a hole in the middle, but to a person who watches them build it, it is a fascinating sight.

Now, I'll tell you how it is built. First, the ants find a place in the ground where they can dig. It is usually next to the sidewalk or in cracks. The ants work hard making a hole in the ground. Sometimes they take out pebbles as big as themselves. In order to shape the hill they take out the sand and pile it on the side.

After the home is built, they store food and lay eggs. The queen lays the eggs. The only way the queen is different from the others is that she has slightly larger wings.

The ants send out scouts. The scouts are much smaller than the rest, or younger, I'm not sure which. One day I was watching an Ant Hill for about ten minutes when a scout found a dead ant. He walked around him for a little while, then picked him up and carried him to the hole about an inch and a half away. This took him about five minutes including rests and more scouting. I call the little ants scouts because they walk around away from the others. No others do that. Every once in a while the scout gets upon his hind legs and turns around as if looking for trouble.

Food is easy to find but hard to get into the ant hole. First the ants drag the dead bug or whatever the victim is over to the hole and take it apart piece by piece. After about one-half hour the victim is all stored away in the ant hill. If the victim has a shell that is the only thing that remains.

Jay ended his report with the advice: "You watch them some day. I think you will agree with me."

The year we were in the 10s, Miss Stall helped her 8s gain knowledge by acquaintance of another kind of organism. According to biographer Janet Browne, Charles Darwin "spent many contented mornings in his kitchen garden imitating the actions of bees landing on the petals of scarlet kidney beans, watching the curly inner pistil bend down to rub the back of his proffered paintbrush and noting how the honey or nectar was placed so that the bee invariably alighted on the correct side. He threw himself into this delicate masquerade with abandon, identifying almost completely with the different personalities and preferences of hive bees and humble-bees (bumblebees)" (1995, 528).

De Lima reports that the 8s talked about Indian beliefs about snakes, visited the reptile room in the Museum of Natural History, and read about the habits of horned toads (1942, 70). Miss Stall then elicited from her class a long list of snake words—among them, *skim, twist, coil, slippery, slimy,* and *rattle*—after which she said: "Finish this story: 'I am a snake. When I shed my skin I...'" Here are three of the endings to Miss Stall's story that members of the 8s produced:

I feel like a new snake. I begin to crawl for the first time.

My body looks glossy. If I did not shed my skin I could not glide along the ground easily. I sleep all winter. I wake up in the spring and hunt for food. I shed my skin in March. I sleep in a rocky cave.

I feel that I am crawling out of an old home. And a little while later I feel the same.

Group Projects

In the mid-1990s, I help organize a symposium on progressive education at a national meeting of the American Educational Research Association. The event takes place in New York City and Kay Kay and Jo Jo come to cheer me on. The panelists are all progressive education enthusiasts, and I anticipate a revelatory discussion. By the end of the session, the three of us are in shock.

Noting in the preface to *The Transformation of the School* that the progressive education movement had "a pluralistic, frequently contradictory character," Cremin wrote: "The reader will search these pages in vain for any capsule definition of progressive education. None exists, and none ever will" (1961, x). Some thirty years later, Arthur Zilversmit nevertheless put forward a definition of a progressive school as, among other things, "one in which children would play an active role in determining the content of their education" (1993, 18). This is precisely the assumption of every speaker in the symposium except me.

The idea of children taking charge of their own learning was a basic tenet of the radical school reform movement of the late 1960s and early 1970s. As we three of Miss Irwin's children tell one another when we caucus after the symposium, it bears almost no relationship to progressive education as we at Little Red knew it.

The other speakers at the session also take it for granted that children in progressive schools do whatever it is they are doing by themselves. These experts give nary a thought to group activities such as the Park School of Buffalo's cider-making, Arthurdale's replica building, the Lincoln School's study of South America, the Shady Hill School's Greeks, the Francis W. Parker School's history of Chicago, and the projects that shaped our lives at Little Red. In the eyes of the panelists, progressive education is ultra-individualistic: it is all about each child having the freedom to do and learn what he or she wants, with others entering into the picture only if one child hurts another or in some other way infringes on his or her liberty.

My classmates and I did not always act in groups. When Johnny was called out in the Stooping Game, he sat down and read a book by himself.

Back in school after our walk around the Village, Olga wrote her poem on her own. We did not collaborate on our spelling and arithmetic tests, either. Yet when I ask myself why we remember Little Red so well, I keep coming back to the fact that our encounters with the cultural stock that our teachers wanted to pass down to us were not just firsthand and in real situations. As often as not they took place while we were doing things together.

The chapter on the 10s in the De Lima book contains a photograph of a play about the Egyptians performed by one of the classes behind us. You can see huge panels of Egyptian-like artwork hanging on the auditorium wall, and you can be sure the play also had music, dance, and a script. Who painted the panels, composed the music, choreographed the dance, and wrote the script? Members of the 10s working with one another. When we were in the 11s, Phyllis and Moyra wrote the preface to "The Composing Stick," George and Moyra were two of the printers, someone else did the cover, and almost every member of the class provided copy.

In a 2013 article on "school turn arounds," the principal of a North Carolina elementary school reported that the teachers held high expectations for all students and "the school also got a facility with more lights and murals painted on the walls" (Hough 2013, 33). At Little Red we were the ones who painted the murals. The De Lima book reports of the 7s: "The group, with every child contributing, has produced two large murals. One deals with farm life, its work and production and pictures a large, fast freight train in the foreground rushing to the city with food—milk, vegetables, fruit, meat. The other mural is a street scene in New York, our own Bleecker Street, where we see a pushcart market, children, babies, taxis, trucks, dogs, the wash hanging between buildings, people on roofs, policemen, fire engines, and in outstanding numbers the silver trucks of the Department of Sanitation" (1942, 63).

As part of their study of the Westward Movement in the 12s, one of the classes above us painted a mural for the school whose subject was "The Pioneer Family." Says Miss Kneeland in the De Lima book:

Sketches are first made in color, and then drawn approximately to scale by the children in their art periods. Anyone who has painted murals directly on a wall can appreciate that it is no small task for four or five children, standing on a long table, to account each for his several square feet of painted wall surface on a panel measuring three feet wide by ten feet long.

Here again arises a situation calling for democratic relations and the appreciation of the ability and work of others. And in this, as in other group work, the backward, the timid, and even those disinclined to participate, for one reason or another, are encouraged to assert themselves. (1942 105)

I did not realize how atypical our school days were until my senior year in college. It is the night before our honors theses are due, and my roommate has practically the whole of Elliot Hall at work in the basement. She is typing away. We are making copies of her graphs, pasting them on the proper pages, and at about 2 a.m. we collate her *magnum opus*. When we are finished, one young woman shrieks with joy: "All of us working together like this. This is so exciting. I have never before done anything like it." I can scarcely believe my ears. The thrills she has derived from this extracurricular and not very kosher activity were commonplace at Little Red.

I once asked my husband to name a gift that Little Red gave us, and he cited the feeling for one another my classmates and I still have some seventy years later. Our group activities may be responsible for this legacy, but from our teachers' standpoint it is not why we went on our trips, put on our plays, produced our magazines, and participated in class discussions. Group projects like these were meant to do double duty: to serve as vehicles for our encounters with academic subject matter and also to extricate us from our narrow cells of personal needs and interests.

John Stuart Mill, the author of *On Liberty* and a man whose paragraphs were often pages long, wrote in *Utilitarianism*, his great treatise on ethics, "education and opinion, which have so vast a power over human character, should so use that power as to establish in the mind of every individual an indissoluble association between his own happiness and the good of the whole ... so that not only he may be unable to conceive the possibility of happiness to himself, consistently with conduct opposed to the general good, but also that a direct impulse to promote the general good may be in every individual one of the habitual motives of action" (1962, 269).

Little Red did what Mill recommended. It used the power of education to instill in us the desire to promote the general good:

> In subtle ways, probably a sense of the whole thrust of the education was in a sense, related to community service. I mean I'm sure I wasn't aware of that at the time. But I think there was a very broad—a very strong sense of community.

> A major part of the experience, was working as a team rather than you know, working against each other.... To summarize, really, it's just all the things that I've said. Yeah. You know, that sense of community, which I think was very strongly developed and was wonderful.... And we accept as part of that sense of community this acceptance of people of all different stripes.

> It was a school that was trying to make people aware of each other that we're all on the planet to get on together.

The group activities that started when we were very young, continued into the 12s and 13s, and ended on graduation day with our choral reading from Stephen Vincent Benet's "John Brown's Body" were one of the main ways it accomplished this. In 1942 De Lima wrote: "Just as in the academic field we speak of teaching children to use the tools of learning—the three R's and certain elementary facts in geography, history, science—so in the field of social relations we may say we are showing children how to use the tools of democracy. Social adjustment does not mean merely acquiring facility in getting along with other people.... It means understanding others, accepting responsibility for them, escaping from the narrow cell of personal needs and interests" (1942, 235).

Fifty years later, the immediate response of one of my classmates to the interview question "What do you consider to be some of the most pressing issues facing us in our time?" is: "This has nothing to do with Little Red." After he is assured that it does, he replies: "I think our whole social fabric is falling apart. I think that's the most serious problem ... there's less sense of 'we're all in it together,' and a lot more sense of each person 'I'm an individual and I'm going to get what I can get and the hell with it.'"

Another classmate reports that when she lay paralyzed in the hospital after the birth of her second child, she said: "How can I commiserate for myself when I know what's down the Hall?" She explains that down the hall there was a ward for babies with rheumatoid arthritis: "And my thoughts were for them, not for me. And I must credit the Little Red School House for that—they helped me think about other people, not myself. I really concentrated on the ills for other people, not my ills. I got through that time because of the Little Red School House."

Whole Person Encounters

Professor Bagley—the man who claimed that progressive education ridiculed the virtues of thoroughness, accuracy, and perseverance, and the ideal of good workmanship—deplored what he perceived to be its tendency to make projects a substitute for systematic learning (Callahan 1960, 351). In 2005, historian Patricia Graham repeated his concern. "If you could demonstrate your knowledge of ancient Rome by building a model of the Colosseum, instead of writing a term paper of its history, you could fulfill your requirements without relying solely on your linguistic skills," she wrote. She added: "Traditionalists wondered what the child had actually learned about Roman history" (2005, 66).

When in the 12s we studied the colonial period and the early United States, Emily and Judy's project was to paint the Triangular Trade on our classroom floor. As Emily approached her 70s she still felt in command of that complex concept. And so, I have had to ask myself what I might have learned—and what I might still remember in my 80s—if I had built a model of the Colosseum in the quite traditional ancient history course that she and I had in high school instead of writing the papers I did.

When I next see my art historian friend who specialized in the classical period, I say: "What would a person have to know or find out in order to build a model of the Colosseum?" "What would the model be made of?" she wonders and when I tell her that I have no idea what materials Graham had in mind, she moves on: "If it were wood or paper you could just carve or cut out the arches. But basically, it's all about arches so you have to understand support and thrust and the relationship between them."

My friend pauses to ponder whether this knowledge belongs to physics or engineering before proceeding: "The Romans introduced the arch and you would have to learn the whole arch form. There were arches earlier in the East but they were mostly underground. The Roman contribution to the arch was revolutionary." "Revolutionary? I never learned that in my ancient history course," I say. "No, they mainly talk about battles. But with the arch you have much larger structures and they were much cheaper and took much less time to build. Did you know that the Romans invented cement? They used bricks, concrete, and marble. The Greeks and the Egyptians only had stone. The arch also meant that structures could be much higher and so contain many more people."

Later I google the Colosseum and discover that it seated 50,000 and that the population of Rome was 300,000. Thanks to Miss Kneeland who drilled us in the decimal equivalents of fractions I am able to figure out that this was one-sixth or 16 2/3 percent of the total population.

When we get to the function or purpose of the Colosseum, my friend talks about its ability to enclose so many people and stresses that it was a theater. "An amphitheater," I ask her? Definitely not, she says and draws me sketches of the two different kinds of structure. "It was a *theater* and it was for huge spectacles. The Romans sometimes even filled the Colosseum with water and put sea battles there." I know about the gladiators, but this sounds so bizarre that I later feel the need to verify what this retired college professor has told me. I again google the Colosseum and of course she is right.

The longer we talk the more convinced I am that to make a model of the Colosseum can be to learn Roman history. Not all of it of course, but a term paper does not encompass all either. You may not learn much about ancient Rome if you cut your model more or less ready-made out of a book. But you will not learn much if someone else has written your term paper for you, either. Before she and I part, we bring the Greeks back into the picture and speculate about how much it would enhance students' understanding if in an ancient history course they made a model of the Parthenon as well as of the Colosseum.

I am not artistically, architecturally, or dramatically inclined and am fairly sure that I never was. Yet I suspect that one reason for the disparity between my recall of my very systematic high school ancient history course and of the social studies we had in the 10s, 11s, and 12s is that in those earlier grades our academic learning was not a purely linguistic or mental process. "If I would fault Brearley, it would be for this," said one of that school's alumnae: "Our education was not for the whole person, but just for the brain" (Fischel 2000, 147).

At Little Red our teachers inscribed our academic learning on our bodies, our minds, our emotions, and ourselves. Speaking just for myself: I wrapped up a mummy, sang about the brickyards, got pricked on my neck by a safety pin as Miss Eastburn helped me on with my serf's costume, mimed adverbs, and spoke one-half of the single line "It's Mistress Winthrop, the Governor's Wife" in our class play about Anne Hutchinson. Putting on my philosopher of education cap and looking back on our teachers, I see that they were doing at Little Red what John Dewey advocated: refusing to divorce our minds from our bodies. What they could not know then is that in the process, they were enacting renowned psychologist Howard Gardner's theory of multiple intelligences before he formulated it (Gardner 1983).

Tribalism Encountered

In writing about my schooldays, I am surprised at how often I use the terms *we* and *us* and how often my classmates do too. I trace this habit back to the fact that we moved through the grades as a group. Our teachers changed from year to year, but we stayed together. Of course one or two new people entered our class each year and one or two left it. But the classes at Little Red were so large—the norm was about thirty-five but in the 13s we had forty-three in our class—that the relatively small changes in group membership did not affect our sense of ourselves as a close-knit entity.

A classmate gives a different reason for our sense of ourselves as an "us": "We always sat in a circle. I mean there were these physical arrangements that I think worked toward community and the group as a whole, rather than the individual. And you know, with building blocks, all the kind of building and structure things we did together, you know, was all very community-minded." Commenting on a reunion of her husband's high school class someone else reports:

> They spent a year finding everybody and so forth, and as a result of that there are a few people who we keep up with, but they tried to have another little reunion and some dinner parties and stuff; it never worked. It never worked because the only connection they had was that they were in the same class and certain fun they had but in terms of them being a community of people it didn't, there was nothing.

There was nothing.... Our class could get together once a year, once every 25 years, as it was, and it was like we never left each other.

Whatever the reasons for our sense of being something more than a mere collection of individuals, our connectedness did not stand in the way of our identifying with our school or, for that matter, our country. Our assemblies and Mrs. Landeck's songs gave us a common culture, and thanks no doubt to the war we were all intensely patriotic. Nonetheless, when groups form, there is always a danger that "outsiders" will be treated badly. "The elementary drive to form and take deep pleasure from in-group membership easily translates into tribalism," says E. O. Wilson in *The Social Conquest of the Earth*: "It is an uncomfortable fact that even when given a guilt-free choice, individuals prefer the company of others of the same race, nation, clan, and religion. They trust them more, relax with them better in business and social events, and prefer them more often than not as marriage partners. They are quicker to anger at evidence that an out-group is behaving unfairly or receiving undeserved rewards. And they grow hostile to any out-group encroaching upon the territory or resources of their in-group" (2012, 60).

Little Red greatly reduced the chances of the translation into tribalism by continually encouraging us to expand our definition of "we." "How could I commiserate with myself when I know what's down the hall?" my classmate asked. How could we discriminate against outsiders when we knew how the Hebrews were treated in ancient Egypt, how Anne Hutchinson was treated by the Massachusetts Bay Colony, and how African Americans were treated in our own country?

Be this as it may, our class was for a time on the receiving end of the tribalism Wilson has in mind:

> We had to walk to lunch every day because we'd eat lunch in a different building—and kids would call us "fairies." We thought that was kind of cute until we found out that it wasn't supposed to be so cute. Sissies, we found out that fairies meant sissies, which meant that we were—as far as I could get it together in my mind—was that we somehow were kind of weak and maybe not as brave as they were because we liked to study different things. It didn't really bother me too much.

I remember having some encounters with public school kids here and there. We played skate hockey in Washington Square and once we were chased out by some tough kids.

I had to walk through Washington Square—well, anyhow, it was an Italian Neighborhood and the kids there would look out for us and say "Ah, there go the little fairies from Little Red." That was the expression. So I was aware. And then sometimes I would play in the park. We called them the "tough eggs." ... Ah, they were tough. They were violent. They wanted your money, or whatever, and you sort of stayed out of their way.

Our big problem was the threatening group of outsiders, the Italian kids taunted us once in a while, or stole our mitts.

We used to march from Bleecker Street to not Charlton Street but near it, a place where we had a cafeteria for our meals, and in the winter time the Italian kids would throw snowballs at us, and on one occasion I guess they even were kind enough to put rocks inside the snowball. And we were strictly forbidden to return fire.

In my mind's eye I can still see the troop of boys running down the other side of Sixth Avenue and taunting us as we walked in line to the playground and the lunchroom. In the 10s Johnny, the author of "Monday," wrote about the "Tough Eggs":

Tough Eggs

One day last summer I had bought a pair of new skates. I went to Washington Square to try them out. It was a very hot day and I was skating down the shady part of the park. I stopped skating and sat down on a railing. A tough looking boy came up and said "Where did you get dose skates?" and I said, "At Wanamakers" and he said, "How much did dey cost?" "Oh," I said, "I don't know. About three or four dollars." Then he said, "Is your father here?" and I said "Yes" but he really wasn't. Then he went away.

A few minutes later I saw him come back with six more tough eggs with him. He said, "Where is your father?" (He spit.) I said, "Over there," pointing to a couple of benches. Then one of them said,

"What's the number of your skates?" I looked at the bottom of the skates but did not see any numbers. The tough egg said that the number of them was on the other side so I had to take it off. He took the skate, said, "It must be on the other because it isn't on this one." So I took the other skate off and said, "Give me back my other one and I'll show you this." He gave me the other one and I said, "Do you want to see my father about them, or something because he's right over there" and I pointed again at the benches. I began walking toward the benches, then I broke into a run for home. I didn't stop or look back until I got home.

I do not recall my class ever trying to solve our tough egg problem. Moreover, until I read the De Lima book, I had no idea that other classes had their own tough egg troubles. In the chapter on the 12s Miss Kneeland tells how one class ahead of us handled a much worse tough egg problem than ours:

> We had been having some trouble, on the way to and from the playground and cafeteria, with some "gangs" along Sixth Avenue. It seemed impossible to establish friendly relations as their number varied from day to day and would, at the most inopportune moments, be greatly augmented. They took to spitting and throwing things at us through the lunchroom windows. Finally Robert and Lewis could stand it no longer and a battle royal ensued.
>
> On getting back to the classroom we took counsel to find out how we could establish and maintain peace and our honor at the same time. After we had discussed the reasons the "gang" might have for feeling antagonistic, Mike spoke up.
>
> "I think I could talk to them. You see, I used to feel just as they do—before I came here. Our gang was Italians, and we used to throw tomatoes and things at the Jewish boys, and they threw things at us. But now I know we're all just the same."
>
> So at lunchtime he, with Larry to back him up, sallied forth. When the rest of us came out after lunch, we found them all sitting out on the steps laughing and talking together. "Porky," one of the "gang," yelled to us, "We're all friends now." And they proceeded to escort

us back to school in great style. With that bunch of youngsters and their friends we had no more trouble. This did not solve all our neighborhood problems, but it did give the children a new point of view and the idea that, perhaps, people could get together if they tried. (De Lima 1942, 104)

Graham's history of schooling in twentieth-century America includes a comment about Little Red by an Italian immigrant woman who lived in the Village in the 1930s: "The program of that school is suited to the children of well-to-do homes, not to our children. We send our children to school for what we cannot give them ourselves, grammar and drill. The Fifth Avenue children learn to speak well in their homes. We do not send our children to school for group activity; they get plenty of that in the street. But the Fifth Avenue children are lonely, I can see how group experiences is an important form of education to them" (Graham 2005, 62).

My initial reaction to Graham's only reference to Little Red was to wonder where the Village woman got her misinformation. "I don't think she knew anything about the school," I said to my husband. "She called us 'The Fifth Avenue children' and in the lingo of the times that meant 'rich.'" On second thought, I wondered how much she knew about her own children's activities on the street. How ironic it would be if her sons were some of our tough eggs. The group activities at Little Red that she spurned included the very kind of discussion that enabled the class ahead of us to solve its tough egg problem.

There is no way of knowing if the woman in Graham's text was related to any of our tough eggs and it is really neither here nor there. Mike, the "go-between," put his finger on the problem. The neighborhood boys perceived us at Little Red as different from them and therefore—just like the Jews his gang used to throw tomatoes at—fit targets of harassment and bullying.

"The wise mother was right," says Graham: "Families traditionally have asked schools to give what they could not give themselves" (2005, 62). One function of school in the United States has indeed been to give children what their families could not.[2] The question is: Which of the numerous educational tasks that families cannot do—or at least cannot readily do—should school take on? The "wise mother" opted for drill and grammar—elements of the warlike pedagogy William James extolled. Little Red's tough egg problem leads me to believe that there was an equally important—possibly far more important—middle-way kind of education that her own children and the others in her neighborhood were not getting.

I doubt that any progressive school or any traditional school when I was young resembled those in the United States today whose populations speak thirty or forty different languages. Nevertheless, and in contrast to our tough eggs, we at Little Red were from a broad economic spectrum and of different races, religions, and ethnicities. On top of this, the acceptance and appreciation of difference was consciously incorporated into the school curriculum, and in our group projects we learned to work and live with one another.

The question remains of whether it was mere coincidence that our tough eggs were calling us "fairies" at the very same time that Professor Bagley uptown at Teachers College was calling the theory behind schools like Little Red "effeminate" (Callahan 1960, 360). Add William James's "soft pedagogics" to the brew and we have what looks like a smear campaign against progressive education. Whether it was intentional or accidental I leave to others to determine. These are, however, genderized terms and they are by no means value neutral. *Effeminate* and *fairies* speak for themselves and *soft* is a code word for *feminine* where *feminine* is understood to be the polar opposite of *masculine*. Just as in mainstream US culture one sure way to discredit a boy or man is to question his masculinity, a sure way to devalue a human activity or institution is to do the same.

A Missed Opportunity

By sheer coincidence, while I am writing this chapter I speak with a group of graduate students at the University of Oklahoma who have just read my *Education Reconfigured*. In that book I wrote that despite the extraordinary amount of violence at home, in neighborhoods, in schools, and in the world at large in the last century and this one, violent behavior is rarely considered to be an educational issue. What can we do about this? These students want to know.

I say to them what I said in my book: we Americans tend to think of school's job as nothing more than the development of mind and to reduce mind to cognition. Of course violence has a cognitive component: the man who beats up his wife and children believes they deserve it; the terrorist who blows up an embassy or an elementary school believes the action is for the glory of God or the good of humanity. But violence also has an emotional component and usually takes the form of bodily action. In many people's eyes, therefore, it is none of school's business.

Our teachers disagreed. Hence Miss Kneeland's effort to teach the 12s a middle way to deal with violence when threatened with it. Had she left her class to their own devices, they might have taken away from their close encounter with "tough egg" violence the belief that the best response to violence is more violence—and that if you do not respond to violence with more violence you are a sissy. Had the 12s already learned that lesson, this questionable ideology would have been reinforced. Instead, Miss Kneeland provided a follow-up educational encounter with tough egg violence for the 12s in the form of a class discussion. This time around they learned that in the face of violence it is sometimes wise to stop, think, and look for a "middle-way" solution between acting as the aggressor did or walking away as if nothing were wrong.

Looking back, I only wish that Mr. Marvin had dealt with bullying in the 10s the way Miss Kneeland handled the tough egg problem for her 12s—as an educational issue. One man in my class tells his interviewer:

> The social structure of the class, among the boys, was very much based on athletic ability, and the ability to fight. Now, it wasn't serious fighting in the sense of, you know, harming anybody but if you wrestled and you pinned somebody down, you won. I don't know that many people ever got really hurt in these fights. They happened frequently. They often happened on the playground. But the pecking order came very clear....When we chose up teams I was either the last one picked or the next to the last one picked, and it was quite clear that nobody really wanted me on their team and it was clear that I was not going to beat anybody else up. They had the power over me. So, I was way down on the pecking order.

Here is what four women from my class recollect:

> This is something that she [the interviewee's best friend at Little Red] still feels guilty about. I can't remember what age it was, probably was around ten, maybe eleven but she decided that she would join

a popular clique and turn her back on me. Whenever this subject comes up, she is just overcome with guilt and I keep telling her to forget it.

I've often thought of [cliques] as very much part of the school.... A very strong, educationally bright, physically sound, and large group of females who dominated and lorded those *way* down below. I tried very much not to be part of the way down below and I joined in terror—always in terror, because I was not like they were, not as they were. But I was friendly with them.

There was a clique ... my emotional memory is that it was forever.... I was an outsider, without question.... And the clique was power.... There was also a thing that I remember of interviewing you to get into this group. Now, I don't know whether you applied or whether the whole thing was part of the general torture routine ... there was a corner [of the playground] where people had urinated, you know, it stank. And the interview was taken—you were in that corner and you were interviewed.... There were two groups of powerless. They were the ones, I guess like me, who were not really tormented that much. We were able to exist except for this thing with this one interview. There were others that were teased unmercifully, they really were baited.

I just know about the cliques among the girls, and there was one that we called the "Put 'Em In and Kick 'Em Out Gang." I don't know if other people have told you about this. I think that's the only clique there was. And it dominated the life of the girls, because if you *weren't* in it, you felt very much left out and you were, perhaps, very much picked on by this gang. I was in the clique. I was not a leader of the clique, but I was very much in it, and I was not kicked out. There were people who were sort of marginally taken in and then gotten rid of and I was not one of those.

My dictionary defines *clique* as "a small, exclusive group of people" and in my memory of the 10s, The Gang was that and more. The classmate who says she joined The Gang in terror reports: "One of the things they did was if somebody did something that they didn't accept as right, as proper, they would—at that time [the playground] had gravel like on the moon—they would take down another female's pants and rub this on her rear end. They were cruel, cruel."

When asked in her interview if she recalled any negative experiences, another woman says: "I think probably the most negative, worst one I remember was when that one student got me in a corner on the playground, and she cornered me while we were there with a bunch of other girls she had sort of gotten with her, and they accused me of stealing. And she made me *cry*. I was *crying*! And she was saying she was having so much fun, she picked me out to bully on purpose and to make me cry."

In 2012, a Japanese young man who read my book *The Schoolhome* in a course at his university sent me a letter. "I'm quite interested in your philosophy," he wrote. "I think *The Schoolhome* can solve lots of problems in education. So I want to implement that in the future. I got a question as I read it. How can you deal with the bully? I think the bully will appear even in the Schoolhome." He is right. Bullying can occur even in a school that emphasizes the 3Cs of care, concern, and connection to others.[3]

A 2012 book reports that in Denmark bullying is "virtually nonexistent": "Typical classrooms consist of a heterogeneous mix of social classes and interests, there is no tracking or other form of ability grouping; and tests and quizzes are not used though grade 6. Furthermore, the use of threats and punishments to discipline and motivate children is relatively absent" (Klein 2012, 223). Danish children tend to stay in the same class with the same teacher for years, their schools focus on cooperation rather than competition, and their classrooms "feature 'a high degree of group work' and the use of 'cooperative projects'" (224). Aside from the fact that we changed teachers every year, it sounds like Little Red. And we had The Gang.

To prevent bullying, an American educator recommends that teachers help students "reach across ethnic, economic, social, cultural, and even gender divides to help them get to know people with whom they might not otherwise speak" (Klein 2012, 240). We in The Gang were equal opportunity bullies. Race was never the issue and neither was religion, ethnicity, sexual orientation, gender, or economic status.

I was a classroom teacher for three years and an apprentice teacher for one full year before that and so I know full well that children can do a lot in school and on the playground that the adults on the spot are not aware of. It took me far too long when I was a fifth- and sixth-grade teacher to discover that one of my young students was extorting money from his classmates. Nonetheless, I am left wondering: Did our teachers know about The Gang and what we were doing to other girls in the class? Did they hope that the targets of the bullying would deal with it themselves? Did they not know that when you are being bullied, this may be the last thing you can do? Or did they think that Little Red was such a safe haven that bullying could not possibly occur there?

One reader of an early draft of this book told me that when she reached the section on The Gang she did not at first believe what I was saying. How could such a thing happen in such a beautiful school? It happened. "Surely," writes the author of a book about bullying, "when students are connected to their schools, excited about learning, and feeling fulfilled by their classes and engaged by their teachers, they will be far less inclined to turn on one another" (Klein 2012, 242–243). Less inclined, perhaps, but groups can form in even the most idyllic settings, and when they do, people can turn on one another.

The wizardry of Little Red was such that even classmates with sharp memories of having been made to feel inferior and of being the targets of bullying report that they loved school. Yet looking back from a distance of some seventy-five years and speaking as someone who was not a target of The Gang but one of its members, all I can say is: how I wish a teacher had intervened! We needed a Miss Kneeland to bring us to our senses, to tell us in no uncertain terms as she did when we were in the 13s that what we were doing was wrong. We needed an educational encounter in which we learned—or were reminded—that the 3Cs of care, concern, and connection (Martin 1985) apply in the here and now as well as in the abstract: to those with whom we live as well as to other races and religions.[4] In other words, we needed a full-fledged class discussion of the kind that one of the classes ahead of us had at June Camp when they were in the 12s:

> It is Sunday evening, and thirty children with their counselors, having finished their picnic supper, straggle to a meeting [at Shelter Rock]. A mock trial is scheduled, half in fun and half in earnest. Some of the boys in the class had tied Larry to his bed, and the class is divided as to the justice of the act.
>
> One of the ringleaders, a twelve-year-old, explains that Larry is a sissy—that's why they roped him up. He likes to dance, spends entirely too much time with the girls.
>
> The argument gradually broadens into a general discussion of the boy-girl problem at this crucial age. Completely oblivious of the

grownups, these youngsters air their most intimate problems. The discussion goes beyond the immediate issues to a review of the group's most serious difficulties during the past year. The children analyze these problems and lay plans for solving them in the coming school year.

For three and a half hours the discussion goes on without flagging for a moment. When the meeting finally is forced to disband because of darkness the children string along the homeward trail through misty woods, still carrying threads of discussion in their more intimate groups.

Shelter Rock brought a rapprochement never before attained in that particular group. Lives were given new clarity and direction. Two years later children were still referring to things said on Shelter Rock. (De Lima, 172–173)

I think it fair to ask if here too the teacher let things go too far. After all, a group of children tying a boy to his bed is no joke. Calling him "sissy"—something that may have been going on for some time—is no joke either. Or did the teacher not know about the bullying of Larry until damage had been done? Be this as it may, early on we needed an educational encounter like the one those 12s had at June Camp.

Notes

1. Or, to complicate the matter just a bit: the learning that occurs in school is a result of encounters with cultural stock in school's *formal* curriculum and also its *hidden* curriculum.

2. For further discussion of this point see Martin (1992; 2011).

3. For more on the 3Cs see Martin (1992, 2011). In 2008, the Buddhist leader Daisaku Ikeda wrote, "The dysfunction so evident in school bullying today thus mirrors the state of adult society, which is replete with insidious forms of bullying ... To surround children with such realities while expecting them to adhere to idealized forms of behavior is hardly fair" (87).

4. The Gang had disappeared by the time we were in Miss Kneeland's class.

5   Buried Treasure

Déjà Vu All Over Again

It is a Sunday afternoon in 1969. My husband and I and our two sons are in Edmonton, Alberta, for the year, and my mother is on the phone wanting to know how her grandchildren are liking school. I tell her that grandson in first grade is writing big *A* and little *a* over and over again. "That's what I did when I went to school," she moans, "has nothing changed?"

So much has changed since that year of big and little *a*'s that if my mother came back as a ghost seeking news of what she loved most, she would scarcely recognize planet Earth. The American school system has changed too. We were given standardized tests galore at Little Red but the school did not measure us by them, it did not evaluate our teachers by them, and its standing was not based on them. As I write, the fate of teachers, principals, schools, and even entire school systems—not to mention the fate of the children themselves—can depend on how well schoolchildren do on these tests. As for standards, of course our teachers had them. Now, however, there are long, complicated, officially sanctioned lists of the knowledge and skills children should acquire at every grade level and the fate of teachers, principals, schools, school systems, and the children rises and falls depending on when and if the standards are met.

Here are a few of the expectations that the Common Core State Standards, issued in 2010 and quickly endorsed by forty-five states and President Obama, hold up for children in K–5:[1]

> Analyze the structure of texts, including how specific sentences, paragraphs, and larger portions of the text (e.g., a section, chapter, scene, or stanza) relate to each other and the whole.

> Assess how point of view or purpose shapes the content and style of a text.

> Delineate and evaluate the argument and specific claims in a text, including the validity of the reasoning as well as the relevance and sufficiency of the evidence.

Analyze how two or more texts address similar themes or topics in order to build knowledge or to compare the approaches the authors take.

My mother would not believe that five- to ten-year-old children are being required to analyze the structure of texts and assess how a point of view shapes style and content. Quite frankly, I am not sure that most of the adults I know—myself included—possess these skills. Nor for that matter do I have any idea why children so young should be expected to acquire them.

The website of the Common Core State Standards says: "According to the best available evidence, the mastery of each standard is essential for success in college, careers, and life in today's global economy." Yet the only careers I can think of that demand the sophisticated interpretive skills set forth in the Common Core standards are those of literary critic and college professor, and I am not sure how many members of these professions the nation can absorb.[2] It is also news to me that expectations like the ones listed above must be met so that a person is *ready* for college. I would have thought they were ones that a student might be expected to meet *in* college. As for the claim that these skills are essential for a successful life today, I can only wonder what kind of life the authors of the standards could possibly have in mind and where on earth they could have found evidence for this astonishing thesis.

The standards have been criticized on many grounds, among them that they make children not want to go to school, are not developmentally appropriate, represent a federal takeover of local classrooms, and indirectly dictate curriculum. I do not know if they have actually undermined local control and made children dislike school. Perhaps these tendencies already existed. That the standards I have seen are developmentally inappropriate and that the whole set of them dictates curriculum seems to me self-evident.

I take that back. *Dictate* is too strong a word. A creative teacher can always devise ways to smuggle in lessons on textual analysis while teaching children carpentry and cooking or having them write plays and set type. But most school people will probably interpret the items listed under the heading "The English Language Arts Standards" as commands to teach English or language arts, the items under the heading "Math Standards" as commands to teach math, etcetera, etcetera. Equally telling, they will interpret the absence of standards for Bach, jazz, carpentry, cooking, community service, origami, ethics, and everything else as commands *not* to teach those subjects.

To date, there have been numerous challenges to both the standards and the ubiquitous testing.[3] I have seen little criticism, however, of the curriculum these represent. Moreover, few seem to notice that the kind of schooling that Dewey and Parker sought to reform has become the default position of both our country's educational establishment and its critics. Yes, the curriculum being imposed on the states is an updated version of the one the US school system adopted in the second half of the nineteenth century when Horace Mann's idea of the Common School became accepted practice in the United States.

Cremin tells us that in Mann's eyes *common* meant free schooling for all children, but Mann's idea of school was also common in that it gave all children the same curriculum. Cremin calls Mann's thinking about curriculum "ordinary enough" (1961, 10). I am not so sure that in Mann's day it was ordinary to prescribe the same curriculum for rich and poor and for girls as well as boys—let alone the traditional academic curriculum for all classes and genders. Nonetheless, this is what Mann did.

If Parker and Dewey came back as ghosts, they would soon discover that today's school reformers are yesterday's traditionalists. One hundred and fifty years later, Mann's curricular thought has been resurrected. The testing and the standards might give public schooling in the United States a brand-new look, but the curriculum they impose is déjà vu all over again. There is a great irony here: we as a nation have never been there and done progressive education but we have in fact been there and done the academic curriculum lurking behind the testing and standards. Not only that. The progressive schools that Parker and Dewey sired were established for the express purpose of correcting that curriculum's significant failings.

As far back as the 1870s Calvin Woodward, a leader of the now long-forgotten Manual Training Movement, criticized the Common School's curriculum for its adherence "to outmoded ideals of gentlemanliness and culture" (Cremin 1961, 26). According to Woodward, the common school's academic curriculum "taught young people to think without teaching them to work; indeed, it actually taught them to abhor work. Ignoring the hard realities of life, it concentrated on aimless, grinding book learning to the detriment of true education" (Cremin 1961, 28).

Woodward's was not a frivolous complaint. The curriculum of choice for US schools some 150 years ago is a direct descendent of the one Socrates's designs for the rulers of the Just State he envisions in Plato's most famous dialogue, *The Republic*. And guess what! That best of all possible worlds is not a democracy. In fact, Plato scorned democracy. In his philosophy, only a select few are qualified to rule the state and those who rule *are not supposed to engage in physical labor*. There is no need to teach them what Woodward termed "work" for it is to be done by others.[4] Besides, they have no time to learn how to work. Plato believed that those who govern should have knowledge of "The Good" and in his view this requires years of intense study of a highly abstract, theoretical curriculum.

To put it bluntly, the academic curriculum Woodward condemned was his era's updated version of one specially designed to educate the heads and not the hands of an elite few. Plato, to his everlasting credit, insisted that just as some men are blessed by nature with a sufficient degree of rationality to govern, so are some women. In consequence, he prescribed the same curriculum for the male and female rulers of his Just State and even advocated coeducation. Woodward's reference to "an outmoded ideal of gentlemanliness" is nonetheless apt. In Plato's political philosophy, the rulers live communally. They have no homes or families of their own, and the children they propagate are reared communally by others. Thus, just as they have no need of an education that prepares them to work with their hands, there is no reason to prepare them for life in what has culturally and historically been considered "women's sphere."[5]

Parker and Dewey went further than Woodward. They condemned the common school curriculum and its accompanying pedagogy for divorcing not only mind from body, but also theory from practice, thought from action, self from other, and school from society. That curriculum nevertheless remained "the" course of study in US public schools until the "curricular differentiation" of the early twentieth century transformed that one and only school track into one curriculum track among several.[6]

Have the critics' concerns been answered? Not yet. Defenders of the old-time curriculum argued at the time that Woodward's manual training was an inferior sort of education and recent enthusiasts have maintained that his plan had untoward consequences for minorities and the poor. But supposing for the sake of argument that these allegations are true, they do not negate the Woodward/Parker/Dewey critique. When a policy is criticized, it does not suffice to show that some alternative to it is flawed. You must show that the criticism itself is unwarranted and this has not been done.

A Case Study of Projection

My subplot about how the delicious lemonade of progressive education was turned into a sour lemon spelled "disaster" has an interesting twist. In psychology, projection is a defense mechanism in which an individual's uncomfortable or unwanted thoughts or feelings are displaced onto another. Incredible as it may seem, this is what has transpired on the group or societal level. Instead of answering criticisms that date back at least to the publication of *Emile*, advocates of the old-time curriculum have displaced its faults onto progressive education.

In *Alice in Wonderland* the Mock Turtle lists the different branches of arithmetic as "Ambition, Distraction, Uglification, and Derision" (Gardner 1970, 129). In recent memory, supporters of the old-time curriculum have uglified and derided progressive education by projecting onto it:

> Uncomfortable Thought (i): The United States has been there and done the old-time curriculum and it was a disaster.

> Uncomfortable Thought (ii): The old-time academic curriculum was designed for an elite.

> Uncomfortable Thought (iii): The old-time curriculum does not prepare people for life in the real-world.

> Uncomfortable Thought (iv): The old-time curriculum was intended for the rulers of an undemocratic state.

In ordinary psychological projection, the unwanted thoughts and feelings tend to be repressed and their displacement onto another is unwitting. A man who accuses his wife of being angry at him when he is angry at her presumably does not realize his mistake. At the group level some of those doing the projecting may be fully aware that they are rearranging the facts even if others are not.

Whether the displacement of the shortcomings of the old academic curriculum onto progressive education has been witting or unwitting, naming it has allowed me to understand why Little Red is missing from the history books. I read somewhere that the targets of psychological projection frequently possess traces of the properties displaced onto them. My guess is that Little Red has been ignored because it so blatantly contradicts the often ugly derisive caricatures. Even the most diehard traditionalist cannot say with a straight face that Miss Irwin's vision of fitting the school to the child was enacted in the country as a whole. Moreover, Little Red's origins, its location, its enrollment policies, and its curriculum give the lie to the charge that progressive education is inherently elitist.

Psychological projection is commonly said to be a mechanism of *self-deception*. The displacement of the old-time curriculum's flaws onto progressive education probably does serve this function. But my long-lasting belief that Little Red had not prepared me academically for Radcliffe when in fact it had simply not prepared me for Harvard's blood, sweat, and tears culture suggests that at the group level, projection is also a formidable mechanism of *other*-deception.

And get this: to shore up their defense of the old academic curriculum and pedagogy, progressive education's critics change the subject. According to Uncomfortable Thought (iii), their cherished form of education does not prepare children *for life in the real world*. The flaw they attribute to progressive education is the failure to prepare children *for the next level of schooling*.

This switch reduces education to a mere shadow of its former self. The Deweyan slogan "Education is not preparation for life; it is life itself" would not resonate with us if we believed that the business of education is merely to prepare children for the next level of school. It is meaningful precisely because we think of education as preparation for life. The change of subject does, however, make me understand the Common Core standards' emphasis on skills like textual analysis that are employed mainly in the academy. Reduce life to schooling and sophisticated academic skills will of course have center stage.

Be this as it may, schooling is by no means the whole of life and few people would call it the most important part. Furthermore, and as Dewey also reminded us, education is for the whole child. Indeed, in the broad sense of the term, *education* is the maker and shaper of us human beings throughout our lives, and it is also the maker and shaper of human cultures.[7]

The change of subject gives the traditionalist an enormous advantage over progressive education in that the old-time curriculum and pedagogy tend to dominate the next levels of the schooling. But an education for heads not hands and thought not action—one that does not even try to extricate children from their narrow cells and is devoid of training in the 3Cs of care, concern, and connection is not—I repeat not—an adequate preparation for life in the real world. How could it be?

The curriculum that progressive education's critics want to universalize was never meant to be universalized. The course of study Plato designed for his rulers is but one track of a three-track educational system. That his system has three separate tracks is no accident. Plato's Just State has three distinct classes—rulers, warriors, and artisans—and the members of each one are supposed to do their own job and no other. Because each class needs a different portion of knowledge, skills, attitudes, values, and patterns of behavior in order to do its own job, Plato outlines a different curriculum for each one.

Add up the cultural stock in Plato's three curricular tracks and the sum total presumably represents the knowledge, skills, values, attitudes, and patterns of behavior that the whole population of his Just State needs. Given that each track transmits a limited portion of the culture's stock, it makes no sense whatsoever to designate one of the three curricula as *the single* course of study for all.

Learning Democracy

In defense of the indefensible, progressive education's critics want us to believe that universalizing the traditional academic curriculum is the democratic thing to do, and on first glance this might seem true. In the name of equality and fairness should we not give the curriculum originally designed for an elite to everyone?

I agree that in a democracy, academic study should be open and available to all. That is very different, however, from saying that it should be *the* curriculum of the nation's schools. Suppose people have different talents or intelligences. Suppose they have different needs. Suppose that the traditional academic curriculum represents a relatively small portion of the culture's stock and by no stretch of the imagination all the important items of stock that the citizens of democracy need to make their own.

Equality in education no more mandates that everyone have the same curriculum and pedagogy than equality in health care requires that everyone be given an appendectomy or a heart transplant because it makes some people well. Nonetheless, defenders of the academic curriculum of yore are apt to tell you not to worry: as long as each new generation of children acquires the 3Rs and their academics, democracy will flourish. They are sadly mistaken. Just think of the many officials in Nazi Germany who learned their academics very well and you will know that the traditional academic curriculum is not in and of itself an education for democracy.

The US school system long ago took on the task of educating its young to be the citizens of a democracy and supporters of the old-time curriculum say: rational deliberation about matters of public policy is the essence of democracy—hence, children must master the standard academic subjects. There is far more to democracy than rational deliberation, however. For starters, it includes the acceptance of both majority rule and minority rights. Even more basic, whereas in an authoritarian system the individual is expected to obey laws enacted by others, in a democracy the citizens or their representatives are the authors of the law. Furthermore, in a democracy everyone is equal before the law, no individual or group is above the law, and citizens are expected to speak out when they do not approve of what their representatives are doing.

Give the standard academic subjects a monopoly over the school curriculum, and the ABCs of democracy may never be acquired. If the educational agents in our society other than school—for instance, home, religion, the workplace, the military, and the media—offered the nation's young an education in democratic living, the failure of school to do so might not matter. But in the twenty-first century they are as apt to instill blind obedience to authority as the basics of democratic living.

Is mastery of the old-time curriculum nonetheless a prerequisite for deciding the complex political, economic, medical, ecological, social, and moral questions of the day? The standard academic subjects shed surprisingly little light on such questions as: What should the United States do about ISIS? What should the nation's stand be on "human enhancement" by genetic engineering? Should the UK have left the European Union? Are our policies regarding climate change adequate? Their answers tend to involve information that is far too specialized and technical to be included in the K–12, let alone the K–5 curriculum; information that falls outside the purview of the standard academic subjects; and value judgments that the various academic subjects try to avoid.

As for the displacement onto Little Red of Uncomfortable Thought (iv) that the old-time curriculum was intended for the rulers of an undemocratic state, this is quite possibly the most egregious projection of them all. One of Dewey's most fundamental insights was that "democracy is more than a form of government; it is a mode of associated living" (1916, 87). Elaborating on Dewey's philosophy, De Lima wrote that the democratic way of life "is not won through shouting pious slogans, through oratory in high places, or even through daily affirmation of its virtues. Rather, it is a slow and almost insensible process built into the consciousness and subconsciousness of our people through a multitude of small and apparently insignificant acts" (1942, 234). As someone who underwent that process slowly and almost insensibly, I can testify that Little Red did, indeed, build democracy into my consciousness and subconsciousness.

Little Red was not a democracy. Few schools for children are. We were not our teachers' equals and they were not our elected representatives. We no more chose them than we chose what to learn. The school did not even have a student government until I was in the 12s or possibly the 13s. I remember that Johnny and I were our class representatives to the committee that wrote the school constitution. But a school does not have to *be* a democracy in order to be a place where children *learn* to live in one, and the student government that was eventually established had relatively little to do with the kind of education for democracy that Little Red gave us. At Little Red we breathed democracy in with the air.

When in the 6s my classmates wash paint jars, make scenery, build Manhattan with blocks, and discuss skyscrapers, they are not only being brought out of their narrow cells. They are learning "the friendly give-and-take" of a "cooperative kind of living" and developing the responsible, reflective thinking that Little Red believed was central to democracy. Of the 6s De Lima says: "The individual's ideas and opinions are respected and the child is free to speak his thoughts. This means also that one child may challenge the opinions of another or question a statement made by the teacher or found in a book" (1942, 235).

Respecting the child's freedom of speech does not mean that anything goes. My classmate never heard the word *nigger* until he arrived at his

New England boarding school. Our tough eggs called us "fairies" but we did not respond in kind. When one classmate misidentified the river she saw from the Empire State Building, Mrs. Hawkins had the group figure out that it is the East River, not the Hudson. Whether we did things alone or in groups, from the 6s on, we were being taught to distinguish fact from opinion and truth from propaganda.

Continuing through the 13s, our group activities also imposed on us the heavy responsibilities to others that accompany the democratic way of life. On graduation day, my class does a choral reading of the section of Stephen Vincent Benet's long poem "John Brown's Body" that begins:

> Thirteen sisters beside the sea
> (Have a care my son.)
> Builded a house called Liberty
> And locked the doors with a stately key.
> None should enter it but the free.
> (Have a care my son.)

At the dress rehearsal, I reverse the words in my solo line and make a hash of their meaning. Mrs. Van Dyke, our drama teacher, is shocked, the class is aghast, and my only wish is to crawl into a corner and disappear. What affects me most as we take our places on stage the following evening is my realization that the success of our entire graduation performance depends on my doing my line—and everyone else doing their lines—well. There is no bailing out. I have to shape up.

Working cooperatively with others toward a shared goal, thinking reflectively about what you are doing, feeling responsible for doing your part well—these were essential elements of our Little Red education. Stop there however, and you could equally well have a recipe for a winning soccer team or a corporate takeover rather than democracy. So, you must remember this: while we were learning to live and work together at Little Red, we were also being made aware of the world around us.

My sons were in elementary school during the Vietnam War, and when I asked their principal if the children had opportunities to talk about the war, she told me: "They are much too young to know about such things." No one thought we were too young to know about war. How could they when it was the backdrop against which we lived our lives! We had fathers, brothers, uncles, and cousins in the armed services. There were war bulletins in the newspapers and on the radio. We saw war newsreels, "The Commandos Strike at Dawn," and "Action in the North Atlantic" at the movies. We listened to "The White Cliffs of Dover" and "Praise the Lord and Pass the Ammunition" on the Saturday night "Hit Parade." And we had Moyra.

The figures I have seen vary wildly, but during World War II anywhere from hundreds of thousands of English children to several million were evacuated from their homes to escape the bombings. Moyra's parents sent her to America to live with cousins—all three of whom were at Little Red.

A television documentary about the London Blitz shows crowds of sleeping people in a Tube station. By the time the blitz began, Moyra was my classmate, but she already knew what air raids were like. Here is what she wrote for "The Composing Stick":

An Air Raid, 1940

It is very lonesome to wake up at about 11:15 to the noise of an air raid siren. The siren blows for about 5 minutes. When it stops it means that the raiders are well inside the county you live in. It sounds like a police siren only louder by far.

Generally people dress and go to the nearest shelter but some stay in bed or go into their cellar or even sit downstairs. We went next door into a cosy room and David and I go to sleep on the couch. David is the son of the people who live next door. We go there because Daddy has to go to the L.D.V. and David's Father to the fire service.

We would sit there and talk and play games or go to sleep until 2 or 2:30. Then to bed until 10.

Chao-li also had firsthand knowledge of air raids. "In my brother's class," one of my classmates reports, "there was a young man named Chao-li. He and his family had walked 700 miles barefoot to escape from the Japanese and he could not speak a word of English when he came to the school." Most of us were spared knowing war firsthand, but we were all keenly aware of the state of the world. "World War II," says one of my classmates, "was a time when Americans were really more united than at any time since then.... There was a feeling that we were all in it together." He recalls that at school "we did things for the war effort, we went out and collected scrap metal and those sorts of things." I remember that we collected paper, tin foil, and tin cans. In addition, we brought dimes and quarters to school to buy the government war stamps that we pasted into albums which, when full, would convert into war bonds.

When we sang "The Peat Bog Soldiers" we knew it was written by prisoners in a German concentration camp:

The Peat Bog Soldiers

Far and wide as the eye can wander,
Heath and bog are everywhere,
Not a bird sings out to cheer us,
Oaks are standing, gaunt and bare.

[Chorus:] We are the peat bog soldiers.
We're marching with our spades,
To the bog.

Up and down the guards are pacing,
No one, no one can go through.
Flight would mean a sure death facing,
Guns and barbed wire greet our view.

But for us there is no complaining,
Winter will in time be past.
One day we shall cry rejoicing,
"Homeland dear, you're mine at last!"

[Final Chorus:] Then will the peat bog soldiers,
March no more with spades,
To the bog.

And here is the poem Phyllis wrote in the 10s:

This War Torn World

This war torn world,
A raging mad tempest
Of airplanes and bombs;
Soldiers, fighting on the front lines;
Bombs shattering houses with a single blow
Wracking cities,

Ruining towns,
Spreading death and sorrow.

Then comes desolation,
A desolation worse than death,
A stillness painful to your very soul:
Nothing, nothing,
Nothing near, nothing far away;
Nothing you can hear,
Nothing you can say.

With every night,
With every day,
You think,
"My end's not far away,"

And then
Oh, painful life!
You do not die,
But live to suffer more.

Your best friend's body
Lies here at your feet:
You cannot mourn
For all departed souls
Who nevermore
Shall live the life
You wish to cast away.
There are too many,
Too many to mourn;
'Twill only laden their poor, dear souls
With a weight
Too great
To hold.

In addition to connecting us to the world outside school, our teachers continually pressed us to expand our definitions of *we*. They made sure that we breathed in with the school air the credo that all human beings are equal, that many are less fortunate than we, and that we need always think about how to improve the lives of others and make the world a better place for all.

Gaining Time by Losing It

I can hear the protests now. Skeptic 1 is saying that democracy demands that every child have a good grounding in the academic subjects. These subjects are very difficult to learn—so difficult that children have to approach them systematically and sequentially. This means direct instruction, drill and practice, disciplined study, homework, and tests. Besides, to learn the academic subjects you must know how to read, write, and do arithmetic; so formal instruction in those must begin as early as possible.

Here in a nutshell is the rationale for a school regimen of blood, sweat, and tears. Yet, at Little Red our academic education began *before* we mastered the 3Rs. We learned about the present, the past, and nature from day one in school, and we did so before the age of television, books on tape, video virtual realities, and Dragon Dictate.

Except for the occasional genius, it takes years of rigorous work to acquire the level of conceptual understanding demanded of a professional scientist, historian, mathematician, literary scholar, or philosopher. But why impose a regimen for professionals on young children? Even those who know early on that they want to enter the academic professions deserve school days that make them happy. They too need to be extricated from their narrow cells and initiated into a democratic way of life.

Skeptic 1 insists that we have no choice: either the academic subjects are taught in traditional education's time-honored way or children will not learn them. Academic learning is like a ladder or staircase and children must climb this step by step: there are no short cuts, it is not fun, and no one can do the climbing for you. You have to climb it by yourself and you can only do so through hard individual work and continuous study.

The ladder/staircase analogy makes one cry, "Aha! Now I see why the academic subjects are so hard to learn!" Yet history, science, math, literature, and the other academic fields are nothing like ladders or flights of stairs. The metaphor applies to the *learning* of the subject matter of those fields, not to the subject matter itself. And here's the rub. The ladder/staircase imagery shapes our thinking. It leads us to believe that the academic subjects have to be taught directly and learned sequentially and cumulatively or they will not be learned at all. But there is no necessity here. School people have simply designed curricula and written the textbooks *so that you have to learn these subjects this way.*[8]

Progressive schools like Little Red knew that the academics that elementary school children need to learn are not intrinsically difficult. They understood that insofar as they are hard to learn it is because *they have been made hard to learn.* The ladder/staircase imagery does not accurately portray the way academic learning *has* to proceed. It singles out one conception of how children's academic learning *should* proceed and obscures the fact that this learning can proceed differently. One of my classmates said in in his interview: "I think that we didn't have the sense that knowledge was categorized. Yes, we had math and we had English, and so on, and we had Social Studies, but they tended to be more integrated and not compartmentalized, and I think that was a valuable piece of learning." I agree.

Ladders can be scary and so can staircases. What if you lose your grip? What if you miss a step? Little Red did not picture academic or any other kind of learning as a ladder or staircase that you have to climb rung by rung or steep step by steep step. It saw no reason to model children's education *in the academics* on an education designed *for academicians.*[9] It realized that these are quite different things and that it is a huge mistake to confuse the two. And so, it taught us children our academics without making us climb ladders or run obstacle courses. And while we were learning the academic school subjects often without realizing it, Little Red's slow pedagogy made it possible for us to become acquainted with democracy as a way of life.

Rousseau said in *Emile*: "The education of children is a vocation in which one must know how to lose time in order to gain it" (1979, 141). Miss Irwin and our teachers were masters of this art, and it was because they gave themselves the gift of time that they were able to give us the gift of democratic living.

In the wonderful hospital memoir *God's Hotel*, physician Victoria Sweet reports that she began thinking of health care at Laguna Honda as Slow Medicine. Although the Slow Medicine consisted simply in a physical examination and an old-fashioned X-ray, it took quite a bit of time. Her daily visits to each patient were not rushed, and the Slow Medicine was conducted in congenial surroundings (Sweet 2013).

After reading *God's Hotel* I began thinking of Little Red's way of teaching the 3Rs as Slow Pedagogy. Our teachers were in no hurry. They read aloud to us every day. They led daily class discussions that made us want to get more information about skyscrapers, American Indians, and the rest. They engaged us in activities such as putting on plays that demanded we use the various 3Rs. They waited until we were more developed both physically and psychologically before giving us direct instruction and drill. And as with Laguna Honda, the surroundings were congenial.

This Slow Pedagogy extended to spelling, grammar, and arithmetic. On the one hand, our teachers delayed formal instruction in them; on the other, they began giving us informal education in them early on. De Lima calls the 3Rs "the tool subjects," and for us they were not simply tools that we would require in some distant future. We needed them in the here and now, be it to read the signs we encountered on our walks around the Village, figure the amount of cloth necessary to make costumes for our plays, build our pueblo, plant bulbs for the school, write the final drafts of our poems and compositions, or find out more about the people and places we met on our trips.

The Italian immigrant woman who believed that Little Red's program was not suited to her children wanted grammar and drill for her children because they were not learning English at home (Graham 2005, 62). Neither she nor Graham, who apparently shared that estimate of Little Red, explains why children who do not learn English at home require grammar and drill in school in order to speak well. After all, children who learn English in their homes do so through immersion, not drill— or rather, immersion plus the correction of mistakes: "The word is '*hamburger*' not 'hangaber,'" "It's called 'Crystal *Lake*' not 'Crystal Lay,'" "Can you say Curious George went to the '*hospital*' not 'hostiple'?"

When I was on the University of Massachusetts Boston faculty, a philosophy student arrived in my office one morning in a state of euphoria. She had just finished a six-week total immersion course in German: Monday through Friday 8 a.m. to 5 p.m. complete with German breakfasts and lunches, German artwork on the walls, German conversation, in fact German everything including the music of Bach and Beethoven. She had started from scratch, she said in awe, and now she could speak German.

Had the Italian woman's children attended Little Red, they would have had an education in the English language that approximated what the sons and daughters of native speakers of English got at home. They would have been enrolled in a nine-year immersion course in English: K–8, Monday through Friday 9 a.m. to 3 p.m., complete with lunch, conversation, lots of singing, and quantities of writing.

In 1942 De Lima wrote: "A school where children are happy, where they are understood, where they dance and sing and paint and play, must be a place, it is claimed where the three R's are neglected, where spelling is 'creative' and arithmetic a forgotten practice" (1942, 214). Says one of my classmates, "We had lots of spelling bees and things like that. And ... the cliché always used to be that if you went to a progressive school you never learned to spell. But we did learn to spell, maybe not everybody, but some of us." The misapprehension survives. In 2011, my friend who went all the way through the Boston public school system expressed her gratitude to her traditional schooling for teaching her how to spell. Then turning to me she said, "You went to a progressive school. You didn't have spelling, did you?"

If you think of teaching as direct instruction and drill and avert your eyes from all the informal education that Little Red was daily giving us in what would now be called language arts and math, then it will seem that Little Red neglected the basics. But that definition is untenable. You can teach good manners by modeling them rather than lecturing about them. You can teach children to love classical music by playing it for them. You can teach someone the love of reading by reading to that person and surrounding him or her with books. You can teach adverbs by playing "In the Manner of the Word." And you can teach children to speak well by providing them with a rich oral environment and correcting their errors. Construe teaching broadly enough to include its infinite variety and it becomes evident that the basics of language and math were woven into the very fabric of our lives in school.

Did the Slow Pedagogy work? The undergraduate education majors who attended a lecture I recently gave on progressive education assured me that tempting as the Slow Pedagogy sounds, they would never use it. Why not? Echoing my University of Massachusetts Boston student who, after watching a film of a British Infant School in which some of the children were reading books on their own, said, "They could never learn to read in a school like that," these future teachers assured me: "Children can only learn to read and write through direct instruction."

A classmate of mine who moved away from New York after the 11s tells her interviewer, "I came from here [Little Red], this progressive education where there were not the rigid forms etc., went to this public school—in Philadelphia so it wasn't the boondocks—and was far ahead of everybody else in my grade level. And could read and write." A woman who accelerated in high school insists that she could not have done so if Little Red had not taught her the basics. The man who was accepted at three New York City exam high schools says roughly the same thing. The woman who moved to the Midwest was promoted half a grade.

A classmate who entered Little Red in the 9s from a traditional public school was by her own account behind in arithmetic when she came into our class: "Well, I felt comfortable there [at Little Red] even though they were ahead academically. Those kids knew things in math, for instance, that I didn't know and the teacher put me in the back of the room with another kid who taught me very quickly what I needed to know to catch up. It was something like long division—there was a particular skill that I didn't have yet."

A man who entered our class in the 13s reports: "The curriculum was much more challenging than in [his former public school]. It required a lot more creative work than I'd had to do.... I don't really remember writing very many papers or anything like that in the [other school]." And then there are the testimonials from Joan and Henry.

By no stretch of the imagination did Little Red's Slow Pedagogy have a perfect record. One classmate has told me that her handwriting has always been atrocious—which does not mean that we never had to practice it. I can still remember arriving at school one morning to see Mr. Marvin putting Walter de la Mare's poem "Silver" on the blackboard. We all knew what to do. Each one of us sat down and copied "Slowly, silently now the moon walks the night in her silvery shoon" in what we hoped was decent manuscript.

Yes, Little Red taught us manuscript, aka printing—not cursive. Horrified grownups—although never my parents—used to tell me that when I grew up no one would accept my signature. I have been challenged only once, and my hassle with that librarian was nothing compared to the amount of time it would have taken me to master cursive and the boredom of the unending drill.

Curiously enough, the cursive versus printing debate has recently resurfaced. Long before the electronic age turned handwriting into an achievement with diminishing utility, our experience at Little Red and the experience of children in like-minded schools put to rest the claim that a person needs cursive in order to be a functioning member of society. Sensibly enough, the Common Core standards do not require it. Several state standards do, however, and other states have enacted laws mandating cursive. Like the patent medicines of yore, cursive, we are now being told, is good for our brains in more ways than you can count. It is, or so cursive enthusiasts say, a tool for cognitive development that raises your SAT scores, builds the neural foundation for such achievements as tying shoelaces and shaking hands, has a calming effect, inspires creativity, and improves your memory.

All I can say is, we at Little Red tied our shoelaces, shook hands, wrote poetry and prose, and got into college without having to devote one school period a day through third grade to learning cursive. The question on my mind is not "Are our nation's young better off if they master cursive?" but "Is cursive writing at risk in this electronic age because the schools in many states are not transmitting this portion of the culture's stock to the next generation?"

It stands to reason that if cursive handwriting is not a compulsory part of the school curriculum, it will not have as strong a lease on life as it once did. But the truth is that cursive is no longer the cultural asset it once was. Being a school curriculum "dropout" does not mean, however, that cursive writing is doomed to extinction. Soon after college, a friend of mine more or less as a lark decided to learn a fine Italian hand—the penmanship style that centuries ago replaced Gothic script and has itself long since been replaced. And so she did. Like earlier forms of penmanship, cursive will sooner or later be considered an old-fashioned accomplishment—one that anyone who wants to and has the time can learn on their own or in the company of friends.

Another woman told her interviewer: "I still don't understand why so many of us can't spell. You know, a lot of us cannot spell, and I don't understand that." I have no reason to believe that on graduation day the Little Red School House class of '43 had a higher percentage of poor spellers than did the eighth graders in traditional schools. My husband's spelling, for one, was nothing to write home about. Once when making out a check this philosophy professor had to ask the recipient how to spell "twelve." In her chapter on the 3Rs, De Lima wrote: "The progressive schools have been the subject of much unjust criticism for the spelling of their graduates. There is a certain proportion of poor spellers in every adult group in college or in life. If any of these have so much as set foot in a progressive school, it makes a magazine story" (1942, 143). I take her point and only wish she had added that there is a certain proportion of people with illegible handwriting too, and also a proportion with serious reading problems.

One of my classmates left Little Red after the 10s in order to be a "guinea pig" at a private school in New York where a pioneer method of remedial reading was being tried out:

> I had a terrible time. I was suffering from severe dyslexia, it turns out, although it wasn't called that then. And I just felt foolish and awkward and I thought that the others were reading—I wasn't reading. Well, I loved Little Red because my mother had gotten in touch with someone called Dr. Orton whom you might have heard of. He was a pioneer in remedial reading for children, and he tested me and found out that I suffered from what he then called Strephosymbolia, which meant "missed signals." I got some letters backwards and stuff, and he had methods of teaching, tutoring me in remedial reading. So, I went to Riverdale Country School because they had a teacher who wanted to learn how to do this the Orton way. And so, I went in as a guinea pig up there—I got a scholarship—and I had also been a guinea pig all summer with somebody; all remedial reading. So, I really learned remarkably. When I was eleven, my reading level went up from first grade level up to, I think, eighth grade level or something. Really amazing!

It truly is amazing. Perhaps there was a magazine story here after all: one about the important contributions Little Red's Slow Pedagogy may have made to her remarkably quick recovery.

School and Home

According to Skeptic 2, whatever academic learning we acquired was due not to school but to the fact that we came from privileged homes. This claim is not new. The Italian immigrant woman seemed to think we at Little Red got everything we needed at home and school simply supplied the frills. She was wrong.

It may well be true that some of us at Little Red learned to read at home. For all I know, some of us may have learned to write, spell, do arithmetic, and become acquainted with William the Conqueror, the Triangular Trade, and John Peter Zenger in our homes or at our local libraries. I, however, had two working parents with neither the time nor the inclination to give me what amounts to home schooling. Many of my Little Red classmates' families were in the same boat and a surprising number of my peers lived in single-parent households. Besides, in 1936–1937 four psychologists spent sixty hours at Little Red observing the behavior of ten members of my class when we were in the 7s and their report, *Child Life in School*, contains detailed descriptions of my whole class during our reading and writing periods (Biber et al. 1942, 55–84).

A classmate tells her interviewer: "I was in a big study that Barbara Biber had done about seven-year-olds and seven and eight-year-olds and their characteristics as learners and as people. And they studied our class. And there were about ten of us who were picked to be studied more in depth. And later when I was in Bank Street now [The Bank Street College of Education] I read the book and of course they changed all the names, but I recognized myself. I didn't think it was too complimentary, but I don't know." "The records reveal a wide range of reading skill," say the authors, "from the accomplished reader who sits intently over her book … to the restless, distractible child who really undertakes to attempt reading only when an adult is right beside him" (Biber et al. 1942, 56).

Seconding the Italian women's disparaging comment about Little Red, Graham writes that the best progressive schools of the 1920s, 1930s, and 1940s were merely "a magnificent supplement to the rich educational environment of their homes and communities" (2005, 66). They were not, however, "a determining educational experience." For the majority of American youth, on the other hand, school "was a primary, not a supplemental, educational experience" (67).

Echoing the thesis that progressive education only benefits the well-to-do, the author of a 2014 op-ed article in the *New York Times* labeled the so-called "balanced literacy" approach to teaching English "an experiment in progressive education," and wrote:

> It plays well in brownstone Brooklyn, where children have enrichment coming out of their noses, and may be more "ready" for balanced literacy than children without such advantages.

My concern is for the nearly 40 percent of New York City schoolchildren who won't graduate from high school, the majority of whom are black and brown and indigent. Their educations should never be a joyless grind. But asking them to become subjects in an experiment in progressive education is an injustice they don't deserve. (Nazaryan 2014, A17)

I beg to differ with the opinion that school played a limited role in our lives. When one of my classmates is asked "What, if any, do you believe to be the long-term effects of having attended Little Red?" she replies: "It is so much a part of the way that I have lived my life, I can't imagine what my life would be like if I hadn't." Explaining that she had "a Jane Eyre-like" experience at her former ultratraditional school another says: "I think progressive education was the matrix from which all of my adult success and overcoming failures stems." At our August 2014 reunion, Olga tells us that Little Red had an enormous influence on her life and the others nod their agreement. As for me, I have for some time now considered my Little Red experience a major determinant of the rest of my life.

I make no claim that Little Red was a primary and determining—as opposed to a supplemental and limited—educational experience for everyone in my class, everyone in the school, let alone everyone who went to a progressive school in the 1920s, 1930s, and 1940s. How could I possibly know? I can only say that it was primary and perhaps even determining for many of us. In the same spirit, how can anyone know that traditional schooling in those years was a primary and determining educational experience for everyone else? Many of my University of Massachusetts Boston students would have said that their traditional school was not primary and determining for them, unless by "primary and determining" you mean "bad." And my reading of Edmundson's *Teacher* gives me the distinct impression that he and many—perhaps most—of his high school classmates would agree.

I take exception also to Skeptic 2's tacit assumption that children who do not come from homes with rich educational environments need a blood, sweat, and tears form of pedagogy. Whenever I try to figure out what made our school days so significant and consequential I reach the paradoxical conclusion that Little Red's environment was the very sort that Graham attributes to our homes. The school's halls were filled with music, its walls were covered with art, the spoken word echoed down its corridors, and the curriculum was shot through with the written word in various historical embodiments. Our teachers read us fairy tales from around the world, poetry belonging to the canons of English and American literature, and novels like Jack London's *White Fang*. We put on plays about historical figures and events. We did choral readings. There were our daily class discussions. How many home environments were then or are now as culturally rich as Little Red's?

Add to this our field trips and school assemblies:

I remember assembly with great enthusiasm.

I think our assemblies was something that impressed me very much the way we sang, and we had speakers who talked to us about other parts of the world and other people in the world.

I loved the group singing. That was wonderful. Everybody in the school, we were all singing at the same time.

Our field trips took us out into the world, and our assemblies brought the outside world into our school. According to De Lima, one day when the 6s were coming home from a trip on the Fifth Avenue bus,

a real cowboy in costume got on. The children were overjoyed and began to talk to him and ask questions. 'Where is your gun? Why do you wear high heels? Why is your hat so big?

Texas Jim [a radio personality] ... was delightfully responsive. He patiently and most intelligently answered all the children's questions. Finally the children begged him to come to school and to bring his guitar and sing to them. He accepted their invitation and the following Friday came for the assembly and sang for the whole school. (1942, 49)

On a trip to the garage of the city's sanitation department, two men entertained the 6s with guitar and banjo. Then the children "were brought back to school in five automobiles belonging to various workers, and there the children invited the two musicians who had entertained them to come back to school some morning and play for the assembly. Several weeks later they did so" (De Lima 1942, 61).

"Woody Guthrie came to your school? He sang at your school? No. Impossible!" exclaims a new acquaintance. Yes, the great folk singers of the day—Woody Guthrie, Pete Seeger, Leadbelly, Burl Ives, Josh White, Richard Dyer Bennett, and John Jacob Niles—all came to our assemblies and sang. One classmate recalls a visit from dancer Martha Graham, and I remember Eugene O'Neill Jr. speaking to us about his father. Then there were our trips to the city's museums—the Metropolitan Museum of Art, the Cloisters, and the Museum of Natural History—as well as to Hoboken, the sugar refinery, and the sanitation department. A classmate has reminded me that we sang Handel's "Where Ere You Walk" at Carnegie Hall. And another tells her interviewer: "I remember I got the mumps ... And I was so upset. I mean, I was really upset because the class was performing at Carnegie Hall—this was on the radio. I was so upset because, you know, I wouldn't have been there singing." Who can ask for anything more?

It is probably true that it is easier for children to learn the 3Rs and their academics if they have an educationally rich environment. But the myth that the schools sired by Parker and Dewey were established by and were exclusively for the upper classes gets in Skeptic's 2's way. *We did not go to Little Red because we were privileged. We were privileged because we went to a school with such a rich educational environment.* I see no reason why all schools cannot have rich environments—which is not to say that they could or should be the same as Little Red's.

Actually, Skeptic 2's sweeping assumption about the homes of poor, immigrant, and minority children—namely that they are not educationally rich—is open to question. Was that Italian immigrant woman's home really educationally impoverished or was it educationally rich in ways that do not count in the eyes of the traditionalists? This question is as pertinent today as it was in the Progressive Era, but if I take the time to explore its ramifications here I may never get to the end of my story. I therefore leave it for others to address and turn Skeptic 2's attention to Graham's remark, "Families traditionally have asked schools to give what they could not give themselves" (2005, 62).

In *The Schoolhome*, I wrote that with both men and women leaving home to go to work an important portion of our culture's wealth—namely home's domestic curriculum in the 3Cs of care, concern, and connection—is at risk of extinction. There is no turning back the historical clock, I said. Besides, women have as much right to leave home each day and enter the world of work, politics, and the professions as do men. Going on the assumption that if home cannot carry out its culturally assigned educational responsibilities, school should step into the breach, I proposed that we turn our nation's schools into "moral equivalents" of home. Here I ask: *If a child's home does not have an educationally rich environment, is not this all the more reason for school to provide it?*

Skeptic 2 has things backward. We at Little Red had such an educationally rich school environment that we did not have as much need for an educationally rich life at home as did children in traditional schools. They were the ones who needed a supplement to the dry, boring, third person subject matter encounters they had in school.

Thinking Outside the Box

In the early nineteenth century, this nation struggled with the question, "Should we have universal free schooling?" By the time my mother was a schoolgirl, that issue had been decided in the affirmative, and thanks to the progressive movement, the nation was beginning to wonder if the academic curriculum that our schools had embraced and the traditional pedagogy that accompanied it were adequate to the occasion. These issues were still hotly debated when I was at Little Red as they again were in the 1960s and 1970s. Today, they are as pertinent as ever, but the projection of traditional schooling's shortcomings onto one of its most promising alternatives has succeeded.

As I write, there is no shortage of educational topics in the public domain: the pros and cons of standardized testing, national standards, charter schools, teacher tenure, privatization are all being aired. The issues that matter most have, however, been taken off the table: (1) Is that old-time academic curriculum really best for all children? Or, to rephrase the question: Should our nation's schools only be in the business of developing children's minds? (2) Is it true that academic learning has to be drudgery? (3) Are humiliation, fear, and intimidation really necessary components of a good education?

One hundred years after the publication of Dewey's *Democracy and Education*, only a nonconformist will dare suggest that direct instruction is not always the best form of teaching.[10] Only an iconoclast will have the courage to cite the valuable knowledge and skills, feelings and emotions, attitudes and values the nation's young are being deprived of because their schools are so intent on keeping their students "on task." Only a heretic will have the temerity to point out that children can get high test scores in reading and math, history and science, without ever emerging from their narrow cells.

My classmates keep reminding me that times have changed since we performed "Thirteen Sisters Beside the Sea," and they are right. Yet, we face exactly the same problem today that we did back then: a world composed of people who differ radically from one another and must learn to live and work together in order to survive. This is where our Little Red experience and the experience of children in schools like Little Red comes in.

Over lunch at our summer 2014 minireunion, Henry wanted to know if there is anything we have in common because we went to Little Red. Phyllis, the first to respond, replied that Little Red taught us to figure things out for ourselves. Then Olga said, "Little Red gave me an approach to life. It's an acceptance of people. It's not just tolerance. It's acceptance of everyone." This brought Naomi to her feet. "Yes," she all but shouted, "and the approach is not about politics. It's a way of looking at the world."

I have always found the last few pages of my books the hardest to write, and here were Naomi and Olga doing my work for me. Progressive education is often associated with the political "left," yet in countless ways our Little Red experience transcended politics. You do not have to be a political liberal or progressive to want America's schools to teach its young to work and live in the world with people of other races, classes, religions, ethnicities, sexual preferences, and just plain abilities. Quite simply, that's the way the world is.

In extracting us from our narrow cells and expanding our definition of *we* to include *all people*, Little Red was way ahead of its times. But the school Miss Irwin founded and I attended predated just about everything now known about the fragility of Earth's lakes and oceans, its ice caps and atmosphere; and also about the rate of extinction of living species other than our own. Whether you vote Democrat, Republican or something else, you can care about the future of life on Earth. You do not have to be a political progressive to agree that in the twenty-first century, schools that fail to include *all species* in the definition of *we* are behind the times—and as E. O. Wilson has said, "all species" does not mean just dogs and cats and horses.

Regardless of your political orientation, you can want a school for your children and other people's children that expands their definition of *we* to include all people, the full range of living species, and Earth itself. And why stop there? Whether you are a political liberal or a political conservative, a political radical or a political middle-of-the-roader, you can want your children to develop their capacity to think for themselves; you can want them to learn their academics without being intimidated or humiliated or bored to death; you can want them to learn how to live and work for the greater good with people who are unlike themselves. You can even want them to have a good life in school, and I hope it is clear by now that I do not mean by this a self-indulgent life.

My father wrote in his Little Red School House *Bulletin* article, "The terror of a child is to be kept home one day; that is the real woe of a sniffly cold." The mother of Niel in my class said in that same issue: "There have actually been tears, concealed but actual when a cold interfered with school, and this same child was discovered two years ago, when attending another school, draped over the window-sill on a near zero day, in the hope that a real miracle might ensue and a cold prevent attendance."

What could possibly make ten or eleven-year-olds distraught at the prospect of missing a day or two of school? I think the answer is that in our eyes Little Red was not our "day job" to which we grudgingly went each morning because we had to. Little Red was our life. The father of a boy some years behind us wrote in the school *Bulletin* about his own schooling: "For us the day began, after five hours of humiliation, when school ended. Then we ceased being so many little robots and came alive as human beings." When, on the other hand, his son comes home from Little Red at 3 p.m., "What happens to him between then and bedtime seems usually to be pretty much in the nature of anticlimax. Which is as it should be." We at Little Red did not have to return home from school to come alive. We were fully human in school. As my father wrote, "The children at the Little Red School House are people, here and now."

Even the most clear-sighted school reformers often forget that to be alive as a human being is to be a member of something larger than oneself be it a family, a tribe, a culture, a community, a nation state. Little Red gave us that larger something. Says one of my classmates: "I always felt that the class, the students in the class, were like a family. We were all one big family." In addition to giving us a family or group of our own, Little Red gave us a world in which to live, breathe, talk, sing, and learn. It was a world so real to us and so vibrant that when we see one another some seventy years later we are drawn back into it.

When in late September 2012 I entertain the Boston area members of the Little Red School House class of '43, Henry brings his songbook. Once upon a time, we each had one of these loose-leaf affairs: two thick slabs of cardboard joined together by hard-to-open rings in the shape of half circles. Whenever Mrs. Landeck taught us a new song, she handed out a sheet with the words and music and stood there while we added it to our collections in more or less alphabetical order. Ann immediately wants to know if "Plantonio" is in Henry's book: "It was my favorite and when I can't fall asleep these days I try to see if I still know all the verses." Henry is not certain, but he leaves the book with me and later I discover "Plantonio"—who, by the way, is a horse—improbably nestled between "Sourwood Mountain" and "Stenka Razin."

During lunch the inevitable occurs and we get started on "The Congo." At mere mention of Mrs. Landeck, Sandy and Henry launch into "Floor, Door, Window, Ceiling" and the next thing I know they are reciting "Thirteen Sisters Beside the Sea." Meanwhile Ann tells us that a recent *New York Times* crossword puzzle asked for the name of the father of freedom of the press. "I knew it was John Peter Zenger," she says triumphantly. When I describe the near fiasco of my Government 1 exam, Olga joins me in singing "Congress Shall Make No Law."

From the children's point of view most schooldays have no rhyme or reason to them: it's Monday, so we have reading and then science; it's November, so we have the Sumerians and cuneiform writing. Our schooldays made sense. They gave our lives meaning. We had a play to practice, a mural to complete, a magazine to work on, a walk to go on through the Village, a pueblo to build, a trip to take to a sugar refinery.

Most school learning is superficially verbal and from the children's point of view it has almost no bearing on real life. Little Red made sure that our learning ran deep by injecting it into our minds, our bodies, and our souls. And because reading, writing, arithmetic, the ancient Egyptians, and the Norman Conquest were integral to the projects we undertook, the relevance question did not even arise.

I recently attended a lecture in which an accomplished Connecticut school superintendent proudly informed her audience that the schools in her system were "data driven." Miss Irwin's book *Fitting the School to the Child* is awash in numbers. Her interest in statistics did not prevent her, however, from founding a school that gave my father such a feeling "of connecting, unity, cooperation in an absorbing enterprise" that he wrote, "I suspect an artist's hand somewhere, an artist in education, Miss Irwin."

In the course of writing this book I have come to think of Miss Irwin as a truly great artist of education. That she was inspired does not mean that we ordinary mortals should allow the school she created and the schools established by the other great educational artists of her era to be consigned to the dustbin of history. You do not have to be an artist to sort through the treasure trove called progressive education in order to see what might still work today. You only have to be willing do as Parker, Dewey, Miss Irwin, and the other pioneers of progressive education did: think outside the box about how to fit the school to the child and not just the child to the school.

Notes

1. At this writing, several states have withdrawn their endorsement from the Common Core. For the most part, however, they have retained standards based on it.

2. Amanda Ripley, the author of the widely praised *The Smartest Kids in the World*, cites with approval a factory owner who says that maintenance techs today have to be able to (1) understand technical blueprints, (2) communicate in writing what happened on their shifts, (3) test possible solutions to complex dynamic problems, (4) troubleshoot and repair major technical systems (2013, 182). I do not dispute this job description. I cannot for the life of me, however, see why Ripley or anyone else would think that the old time academic curriculum would prepare people to fill it.

3. See, for example, Diane Ravitch's speech to the Modern Language Association, January 11, 2014 (Strauss 2014; cf. Kirp 2014).

4. Schultz (2001) says in his review of *Left Back*: "Ravitch cannot see the relationship of work to citizenship. Neither could Plato but in his case this does not matter for in his philosophy those who worked were not full-fledged citizens. In Ravitch's case it does matter for she is talking about the education of the citizens in a democracy."

5. For a fuller discussion of Plato's educational philosophy, see Martin (1985).

6. The manual training Woodward wanted to introduce into the school curriculum was not meant to be vocational, nor was it intended to be a separate curriculum track. Supporters

of the standard academic school curriculum loudly criticized the Manual Training Movement for seeking to develop children's "lower faculties."

7. For more on this point, see Martin (2011).

8. Even if it is true, as some critics say, that these fields have an "internal logic," that logic would not dictate the way they should be *learned*.

9. Actually, it is not obvious that the ladder imagery holds for them either.

10. Progressive schools do of course exist, but mainstream discussions of education pay little if any attention to their practices.

Epilogue

On a sunny day in July 2015, I drive with a college friend to the Ball Lake Dam in Vermont. "It's not the size of the Hoover Dam," she cautions me, "but it's a real dam." I am prepared for a small pile of rocks and arrive instead at an engineering feat that provides close to one thousand homes with electricity. I read about the TVA in college and not too long ago saw a public television documentary on the Hoover Dam, but never before have I had knowledge by acquaintance of a real live government-built dam.

To my astonishment, this field trip turns into a lesson as powerful for me at age 86 as the trip to the top of the Empire State Building was for my class in Mrs. Hawkins's 6s. Sitting in a circle back at 196 Bleecker Street, they figured out the location of the Hudson and the East Rivers, and after a brief excursion to a construction site, they discussed how skyscrapers are made. Standing at the dam, my friend and I talk about the Connecticut and the West Rivers and how waterpower is transformed into electricity.

Critics of progressive education tend to view field trips as "add ons" to the school curriculum: "frills" they call them or "enrichment." Those who sired the progressive schools of yore like Little Red believed to the contrary that children need firsthand experience of the world they live in. In an age when both children and adults are tethered to iPhones, iPads, and laptops, I can only agree. And I would go further.

In 2013 the in-house magazine of the retirement community in which I live published a poem by DD Abeles:

<u>Marks</u>

A pencil can record a thought
Make a sum of what you bought
Draw a picture of a place
All these you can erase,
But what is written in the heart
Will forever stay in place.

My close encounter with the Lake Ball Dam leads me to believe that the field trips we took at Little Red go far to explaining why the schooldays of us lucky ones are still written in our hearts.

Had the Lake Ball Dam been built when we were in the 6s and Little Red been located in Vermont instead of Greenwich Village, Mrs. Hawkins might have taken us there. Safely back in school, she would have asked us: Where exactly did the West River flow before it was dammed up? Who do you think built the dam? How do you think they did it? With an older group of children she might have put the questions: Were people displaced? What was life like in Vermont before the dam was built? All of which is to say that an entire curriculum can be built around a field trip.

I cannot stress too much, however, that as the world changes, so do the questions that a field trip inspires. Mrs. Hawkins did not ask my class what the building of skyscrapers did to the natural environment. In 1934 or 1935, the possibility of whole habitats being destroyed would not have occurred to her. In 2015, the issue of how a construction project that is designed to benefit us humans affects the rest of the living world looms large.

And now it is Skeptic 3's turn. You are a utopian dreamer, he or she will say. Field trips take time, and children in the twenty-first century have none to spare. In your day, there was much less knowledge for young people to acquire and life was not nearly so pressured as it is now. If today's children do not buckle down at an early age and forego the frills, they and the entire country will be left behind. Skeptic 3's scenario of pressure cooker schools for a pressure cooker world is being enacted as I write. Four days after my field trip to the Lake Ball Dam, a *New York Times* columnist lamented how stressed out high school students are today and cited with approval a *Time* magazine article that says, "There has to be a place where kids can breathe" (Bruni 2015, A19). The pressure on children in K–8 is undoubtedly less than on those in 9–12, but pressure there nonetheless is.

Claims that take the form "Society has characteristic X; ergo school must have characteristic X" are, however, invalid. There is a great deal of violence in society in the United States today. Does this mean that there should also be a great deal of violence in our schools? Of course not. Murder, rape, racism, and homophobia exist in society today. Does it follow that these practices should exist in the nation's schools? Not at all. Thus, even if one agrees with Skeptic 3 that US society today is more highly pressured than it was during the Great Depression and World War II, it does not follow that school should be more pressured than then.

School environments do not mirror society, and I can think of no good reason why they should. In school, my classmates and I walked down the streets of New York in a line and with a partner. People in the "outside" world did not do this. On the other hand, some of those people must have been calling us "fairies" in earshot of their children—how else would our tough eggs have thought to do so? We, however, did not use such language in school. The fact is that school is highly selective in both its practices and its taboos. Thus, it has a choice. It can copy society in making its inhabitants feel pressured; it can outdo society in this respect; and if it wants to and has sufficient determination, it can instead create an environment in which children can breathe.

Miss Irwin created an environment in which we children did more than simply breathe. My hope is that every child in this country—in fact, every child in the world—will one day soon be as lucky as my classmates and I were. Utopian dreamer that I no doubt am, my great wish is that every school in the world will give its children the gift that Little Red gave us—the one still written in my heart—of a good life filled with both learning and an ever-expanding definition of *we*.

Bibliography

Alcott, Louisa M. 1936. *Little Women*. Boston: Little, Brown.

Anderson, Melinda B. 2015. "Where Teachers Are Still Allowed to Spank Students," *The Atlantic.com*, December 15.

Bagley, William. 1960. "The Essentialist Philosophy of Education." In *An Introduction to Education in American Society*, edited by Raymond Callahan, 346–361. New York: Knopf.

Biber, Barbara, Lois B. Murphy, Louise P. Woodcock, and Irma S. Black. 1942. *Child Life in School*. New York: E. P. Dutton.

Bronte, Charlotte. 1997. *Jane Eyre*. New York: Signet.

Browne, Janet. 1995. *Darwin Voyaging*. Princeton: Princeton University Press.

Bruni, Frank. 2015. "Today's Exhausted Superkids," *New York Times*, July 29, A19.

Butche, Robert. 2000. "A monochromatic view of the colorful history of education." Review of Diane Ravitch Left Back, November 2. Amazon.com.

———.2000. *Image of Excellence*. New York: Peter Lang.

Chapman, Robert L., ed. 1986. *The New Dictionary of American Slang*. New York: Harper & Row.

Christie, Agatha. 1972. *Elephants Can Remember*. New York: Dell.

Cremin, L. 1961. *The Transformation of the School*. New York: Knopf.

Cuban, Larry. 1993. *How Teachers Taught*, 2nd edition. New York: Teachers College Press.

De Lima, Agnes. 1942. *The Little Red School House*. New York: Macmillan.

De Lima, Agnes, Baxter Tompsie, and Thomas J. Francis. 1942. *South of the Rio Grande: An Experiment in International Understanding*. New York: Bureau of Publications, Teachers College, Columbia University.

Denby, David. 2012. "Public Defender," *New Yorker*, November 19: 66–75.

Dewey, John. 1938. *Experience and Education*. New York: Collier Books.

———. 1956 [1899]. *The School and Society*. Chicago: University of Chicago Press.

———. 1961 [1916]. *Democracy and Education*. New York: MacMillan.

Dewey, John, and Evelyn Dewey. 1915. *Schools of Tomorrow*. New York: E. P. Dutton.

Dillon, Sam. 2011. "Civics Education Called National Crisis," *New York Times*, May 5, A21.

Edmundson, Mark. 2002. *Teacher*. New York: Random House.

Eisenstein, Elizabeth. 1980. *The Printing Press as an Agent of Change*. Cambridge: Cambridge University Press.

Engel, Mimi, Amy Claessens, Tyler Watts, and George Farkas. 2016. "Mathematic Content Coverage and Student Learning in Kindergarten." *Educational Researcher*, 45, no. 5: 293–300.

English Language Standards. Common Core State Standards Initiative, corestandards.org.

Fallace, Thomas, and Victoria Fantozzi. 2013. "Was There Really a Social Efficiency Doctrine? The Uses and Abuses of an Idea in Educational History," *Educational Researcher*, 42, no. 3: 142–50.

Fishel, Elizabeth. 2000. *Reunion*. New York: Random House.

Freed, Florence. 2007. "The Trading Cards," *The Lincoln Review*, March–April.

Gardner, Howard. 1983. *Frames of Mind*. New York: Basic Books.

Gardner, Martin. 1970. *The Annotated Alice*. London: Penguin Books.

Goodwin, Doris Kearns. 2013. *The Bully Pulpit*. New York: Simon and Schuster.

Graham, Patricia Albjerg. 2005. *Schooling America*. Oxford: Oxford University Press.

Hampton, Dina. 2013. *Little Red*. New York: Public Affairs.

Hirsch, E. D., Jr. 1987. *Cultural Literacy*. Boston: Houghton Mifflin.

Hirsch, E. D., Jr., Joseph F. Kett, and James Trefil. 1998. *The Dictionary of Cultural Literacy*. Boston: Houghton Mifflin.

Hoffman, Eva. 1989. *Lost in Translation*. New York: Penguin Books.

Hough, Lory. 2013. "Turnaround Time," *Ed. Harvard Graduate School of Education*, Summer, 33.

Hylton, Wil S. 2014. "Unbeakable," *New York Times Magazine*, December 18: 36–43.

Ikeda, Daisaku. 2008. *Embracing the Future*. Tokyo: The Japan Times.

Ingraham, Christopher. 2016. "The States Where Teachers Still Beat Kids," *The WashingtonPost.com*, January 14. *https://www.washingtonpost.com/news/wonk /wp/2016/01/14/the-states-where-teachers-still-beat-kids/?utm_term=.b585ca6c0310*.

Irwin, Elisabeth. 1932. "A Real-Life Plan," *New York Times*, May 15.

Irwin, Elisabeth A., and Louis A. Marks. 1924. *Fitting the School to the Child*. New York: Macmillan.

James, William. 1958. *Talks to Teachers*. New York: W.W. Norton.

Kaplan, Judy, and Linn Shapiro. 1998. *Red Diapers*. Urbana, IL: University of Illinois Press.

Keller, Evelyn Fox. 1985. *Reflections on Gender and Science*. New Haven: Yale *University Press*.

Kirp, David L. (2014). "Rage Against the Common Core," *New York Times*, December 28: SR19.

Klein, Jessie. 2012. *The Bully Society*. New York: New York University Press.

Knapp, Liza. 2004. "What Was on Tolstoy's Bookshelf?" *Oprah.com*, May 31.

Knoll, Michael. 2012. "'I Had Made a Mistake': William H. Kilpatrick and the Project Method," *Teachers College Record*, February, 144, no. 2.

Krugman, Paul. 2013. "Errors and Lies," *New York Times*, May 18: A17.

Lehrer, Jonah. 2012. "Kin and Kind," *New Yorker*, March 5: 36–42.

Mann, Thomas. 1996. *The Magic Mountain*. Translated by John E. Woods. New York: Vintage Books.

Mannheim, Karl. 1996. "On the Problem of Generations." In *Theories of Ethnicity*, edited by Werner Sollors. New York: New York University Press, 109–55.

Martin, Jane Roland. 1985. *Reclaiming a Conversation*. New Haven: Yale University Press.

———. 1992. *The Schoolhome*. Cambridge: Harvard University Press.

———. 1994. *Changing the Educational Landscape*. New York: Routledge.

———. 2000. *Coming of Age in Academe*. New York: Routledge.

———. 2002. *Cultural Miseducation*. New York: Teachers College Press.

———. 2007. *Educational Metamorphoses* Lanham, MD: Rowman & Littlefield.

———. 2011. *Education Reconfigured*. New York: Routledge.

Mayer, Jane. 2016. *Dark Money*. New York: Anchor.

Mill, J. S. 1962. *Utilitarianism, on Liberty, Essay on Bentham*. New York: New American Library.

Mirrel, Jeffrey. 2006. "The Traditional High School," *Education Next*, 6, no. 1.

Mishler, Paul C. 1999. *Raising Reds*. New York: Columbia University Press.

Mori, Kyoko. 1997. *Polite Lies*. New York: Fawcett Books.

Moyers, Bill. 2004. *Moyers on America*. New York: New Press.

Nazaryan, Alexander. 2014. "The Fallacy of 'Balanced Literacy'," *New York Times*, July 7: A17.

Newman, Joseph W. 1999. "Experimental School, Experimental Community: The Marietta Johnson School of Organic Education in Fairhope, Alabama." In *"Schools of Tomorrow," Schools of Today*, edited by Susan F. Semel and Alan R. Sadovnik. New York: Peter Lang.

New York Times. "Depression to Halt School Experiment." March 26, 1932.

———. "Start Move to Save 'Little Red School'," April 10, 1932.

———. "Aid 'Little Red School'," April 15, 1932.

———. "New and Old Clash at Public School 41," May 1, 1932.

———. "'Little Red School' Saved by Teachers'," May 12, 1932.

Ohan, Nicholas. 2009. "The Little School That Could." *Independent School*. National Association of Independent Schools Online Feature.

O'Hara, R. J. 2001. "Romping through a Hundred Years of Educational Folly." Review of Diane Ravitch Left Back. August 8. Amazon.com.

Class of 1938, Ohio State University. 1938. *Were We Guinea Pigs*? New York: Holt.

Orwell, George. 1984. "Such, Such Were the Joys" in *The Orwell Reader*. New York: Harcourt, Brace.

Paul, Pamela. 2013. "Reading, Writing and Video Games," *New York Times*, March 17: SR4.

Perlstein, Daniel, and Sam Sack. 1999. "Building a New Deal Community: Progressive Education at Arthurdale." In *"Schools of Tomorrow," Schools of Today*, edited by Susan F. Semel and Alan R. Sadovnik, 213–238. New York: Peter Lang.

Pinker, Steven. 2002. *The Blank Slate*. New York: Viking.

Plato. 1974. *The Republic*. Translated by G. M. A. Grube. Indianapolis: Hacket.

Provenza, Eugene F. Jr. 1999. "An Adventure with Children." In *"Schools of Tomorrow," Schools of Today*, edited by Susan F. Semel and Alan R. Sadovnik, 103–120. New York: Peter Lang.

Rao, Anthony. 2014. Letter to Editor. *New York Times*, September 14: A20

Ravitch, Dianne. 2000. *Left Back*. New York: Simon & Schuster.

Ravitch, Dianne. 2013. *Reign of Error*. New York: Vintage.

Ravitch, Diane. 2014 "Common Core Standards: Past, Present, Future." Chicago: Speech to Modern Language Association.

Reese, William J. 2013. "The First Race to the Top," *New York Times*, April, 21: SR8.

Ripley, Amanda. 2013. *The Smartest Kids in the World*. New York: Simon & Schuster.

Rosenthal, Neil. 2005. "Article Review: A Matter of Opinion by Victor S. Navasky," *Commentary*, September.

Rousseau, J. 1979 . *Emile*. Translated by Allan Bloom. New York: Basic Books.

Schultz, Andrew E. 2001. "Review of Ravitch, D. (2000). *Left Back*." *Digital Library and Archives*, 38, no. 2.

Shaker, Paul. 2004. *"Left Back*: Punditry or History?" *Journal of Curriculum Studies*, 36, no. 4: 495–507.

Stein, Jess. 1980. *The Random House Dictionary*. New York: Ballantine Books.

Sweet, Victoria. 2013. *God's Hotel*. New York: Riverhead Books.

Strauss, Valerie. 2014. "Everything You Need to Know about Common Core—Ravitch," *Washington Post.com*, January 18.

Tey, Josephine. 1950. *Brat Farrar*. New York: Scribner.

———. 1951. *The Daughter of Time*. New York: Scribner.

Tyack, David B. 1974. *The One Best System*. Cambridge, MA: Harvard University Press.

Tyack, David, and Larry Cuban. 1995. *Tinkering Toward Utopia*. Cambridge, MA: Harvard University Press.

Wilson, Edward O. 2012. *The Social Conquest of the Earth*. New York: Liveright.

Zilversmit, Arthur. 1993. *Changing Schools*. Chicago: University of Chicago Press.

Index

JANE ROLAND MARTIN is Professor of Philosophy Emerita at the University of Massachusetts, Boston. She is the author of nine books, including *Reclaiming a Conversation, The Schoolhome, and Education Reconfigured*, and is the winner of numerous honors, among them fellowships from the John Simon Guggenheim Memorial Foundation and the MacDowell Colony and the 2013 Outstanding Career Achievement Award from the John Dewey Society.

CPSIA information can be obtained
at www.ICGtesting.com
Printed in the USA
BVHW03s1715090418
512869BV00001B/39/P